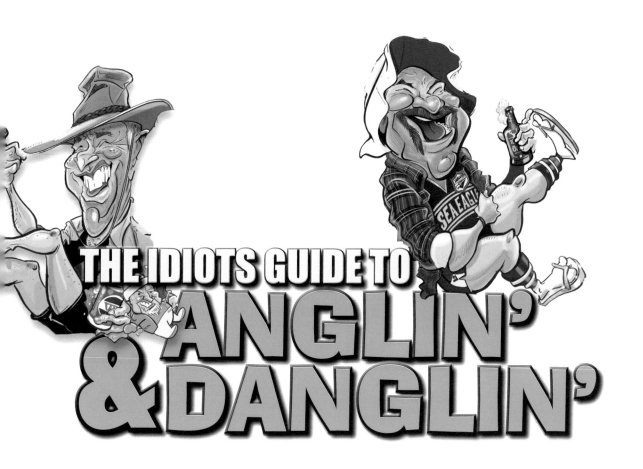

THE IDIOTS GUIDE TO ANGLIN' & DANGLIN'

A FISHING MANUAL FROM TWO OF
AUSTRALIA'S FAVOURITE SONS...
BARRY JEFFREYS & ROY McCOY

Played by Terry Daniher & Anthony "Lehmo" Lehmann

Written & Created by Drew Howell
Illustrated by Michelle Yann

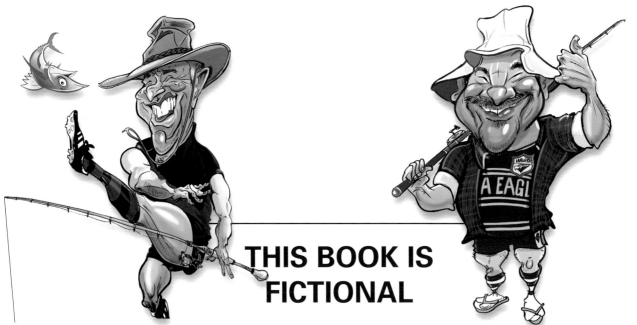

THIS BOOK IS FICTIONAL

Some real events and names have been used in creating context and backdrop for the characters.

First Published 2020

Published and distributed by
Australian Fishing Network
PO Box 544 Croydon, Victoria 3136
Telephone: (03) 9729 8788   Facsimile: (03) 9729 7833
Email: sales @ afn.com.au   Website: www.afn.com.au

ISBN: 9781 8651 3392 8

LIST OF CHAPTERS

BARRY JEFFREYS

- born 1958 -

A young Barry practising the 2 handed whip cracking technique which would later become his signature move as one of Australia's top celebrity fishermen

Hometown: Gunpowder, QLD
Angler/Dangler:
Whatever conditions call for
Known for: His signature 2 handed whip cracking technique and tellin' a good yarn
Headwear: Bucket hat
Career Avg: 5.7 legal fish per trip
Strike Rate: every 42 mins
Highest Score: 49

casting forever.

Back to the farm for another 3 painstaking years on his fathers orders, Barry was finally allowed to follow his dream, and that he did, fishing the coastal and inland waters of Australia and the world for the next four decades.

Born and raised in the small town of Gunpowder, north of Mt. Isa in Central QLD, it is fair to say Barry Jeffreys stance amongst the fishing elite was hardly a natural progression. It wasn't until 1968 at the budding age of 15 that Barry's natural but *extraordinary casting abilities* were discovered by a lost travelling fisherman on the family's farm. For years Barry's *two handed whip cracking technique* was ridiculed by locals until at last the fisherman saw in Barry a rarity that not many possess and convinced his father to allow the boy to travel to *Bald Knob, QLD* to compete in the Annual Longest Cast Competition. It was the first time Barry had seen an expanse of water larger than a bath tub, and in one single flick of his wrists he not only took the title and smashed the record, but had revolutionised

Barry with his beloved Gunpowder Magpies. They would play league on Saturday morning, union in the arvo and then back-up in Aussie Rules on the Sunday... in the same kit!

Barry was born to farm the land, but chose the bright lights of football, sailing the high seas and fishing stardom.
Here he is with his first pride and joy... the Cortina

Barry's sporting prowess was further established in 1972 when he stormed the last round of the famous **Thong Throwing Competition at Whyalla**, taking home the coveted **Golden Thong Award.**

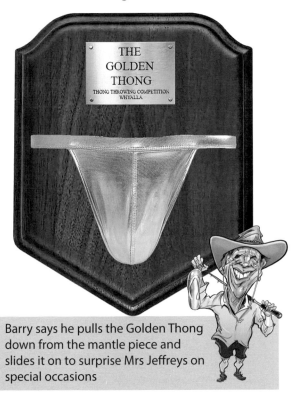

Barry says he pulls the Golden Thong down from the mantle piece and slides it on to surprise Mrs Jeffreys on special occasions

Barry looked so much like the Daniher boys Sheeds thought he was one of the brothers

Left to right: Anthony Daniher, Barry Jeffreys, Neale Daniher and Chris Daniher

Not only was he handy with a thong in hand, but turns out Big Barry wasn't bad with a Sherrin in hand either and was drawn down to Windy Hill by Kevin Sheedy to don the sash for the **Essendon Football Club** in the **VFL**. Years later he was joined at the Bombers by 3 brothers - the **Danihers** - that eerily looked much like him, so much so, Sheeds coined them **'the 4 brothers'**. Baz got 2 premierships with the Bombers and had a stellar career.

Barry used to show up at Daniher family functions for a laugh...
Left to right: Neale Daniher, Anthony Daniher, Edna Daniher, Jim Daniher, Chris Daniher... and Barry Jeffreys

Someone once said, "the celebrations often outweigh the event."
That might have been Baz
Half time, Rd 1, 1985

Triumph '83

AMERICA'S CUP

Australia 36c

ESSENDON

NUBRIK

133 of 156

BARRY JEFFREYS

Barry was a loyal servant to the Bombers

His rise to celebrity wasn't complete until he became a member of the victorious **1983 America's Cup** crew.

Barry convinced owner **Alan Bond** and Skipper **John Bertrand** that a full-time fisherman on - board would keep the crew well nourished and was later credited by the two as "being a genius" for giving his crew the winning advantage. Many cynic's of this revolutionary position in a sailing crew believe the twin keel design of **Ben Lexcen's Australia II** was to thank, however Barry and those who got to drink from the cup and become the toast of the nation know the truth.

Barry reinvented sailing and has the medal to prove it.
1983 America's Cup Winner's Medal

Barry 'the sailing fisherman' celebrating on board Australia II, 1983 America's Cup victory.
Who would've thought the boy from Gunpowder would be rubbing shoulders with 'millionaires' in Sailing Clubs

A matter of fate was the union of Barry with soon to be lifelong friend Roy McCoy on that very voyage. Barry introduced Roy to fishing and the two have shared this bond for many years.

Barry receiving the Award for Most Valuable Crew Member on-board Australia II.
Apparently he won a lifetime supply of beer.
Was around the time he and Roy became close...

Just a couple of Celebrity Fishermen on a boat.
Roy & Barry circa 1997

Barry just bein' Barry

He has gone on to write many books including; **What's Cookin' Good Hookin', and Bringin' Home the ~~Bacon~~ Fish.**

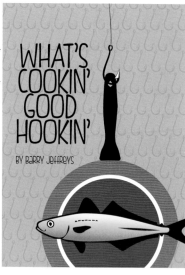

WHAT'S COOKIN' GOOD HOOKIN'

BY BARRY JEFFREYS

He also worked on **"Escape with ET"** as ET's personal fishing double and tells us he got the fish on the line before the younger, more camera friendly ex-shark would step in for the screen.

With an A-list of friends all waiting for their invite for a day on the high seas, Barry is firmly in the who's who of Australian fishing celebrity, and is the deserved five time recipient of the **Australian Association of Ex-Sportmen Turned Celebrity Fisherman (AAESTCF)** of the year, topped only by **ET** himself.

Two of the great Australian Ex-Sportsmen Turned Celebrity Fishermen. *ET & Barry on set during filming of ET's fishing show circa 2003*

ROY McCOY

- born 1961 -

Age: 54
Hometown: Eggs and Bacon Bay, TAS
Angler/Dangler:
Devout angler… unless employing the toe pull method after a few beers
Preferred fishing attire: Stubbies and flannel
Career Avg: 11 tinnies per trip
Strike Rate: 1 tinny every 13mins
Highest Score: 49 in one outing – 3 short of David Boon's record

I ntroducing the man, the myth, the legend, **Mr Roy McCoy.**

Recently admitted to The Aussie Battlers Hall of Fame, Roy McCoy has become a household name. Always one for a laugh and not shy of making himself the centre of public amusement, with Roy comes precision, dedication and excellence… or something like that. Either way, you're sure to have a good time.

Growing up in the deep south of Tasmania, Roy was son to local sporting legends Reg and Joy McCoy, so it became no surprise when he burst onto the Australian sporting scene. Reg and Joy themselves have over 90 marathons between them, and were the first couple to play in a (then) **VFL Grand Final** in Collingwood's 1956 loss to Melbourne in front of 116,002 fans.

The front page of The Melbourne paper from 1956 showing the crowd that came out to see Reg and Joy for the Pies in the VFL Grand Final

They also went on to be the successful opening batting pair for the Tasmania Cricket Association's **'55/'56 Premiers** Glenorchy, their marriage coming under strain that season after Reg ran Joy out in the final. Joy took revenge the next month in the annual North versus South representative match, by calling Reg through for a single that was never there whilst he was on 99. Marriage counselling and coach intervention thankfully brought the couple back together for the 56/57' season.

Joy re-enacting the run out that led to her and Reg's marital breakdown in the marriage counsellors office… it doesn't look like Reg is enjoying re-living the moment

Following in their footsteps, Roy had represented Tasmania in Athletics, Swimming, Australian Rules, Rugby

League, Rugby Union, Cricket, Sailing, Fencing, Dodgeball, Marbles, Chess, Connect 4, Debating, Poetry Recital and as a soprano in The Tasmanian Chorale by the tender age of 11.

Roy's bonanza year of **'83** included both the **VFL and NSWRL Grand Finals.**

Well that's not exactly how it played out...

Roy's singing career was nearly brought to a halt after copping one in the plums at cricket training. Meant he just had to join the Castratos until the swelling went down

A young Roy honing his craft at swimming practice

After a little sleep over to calm the nerves before the big dance, Roy didn't quite make it to the "G" for that last Saturday in September. His car breaking down on a country road en-route, meaning he missed game time and the **VFL** Premiership for his beloved **Hawthorn**.

The **Hawks** went onto belt Barry's **Bombers** without him and Roy was left lamenting what could have been... as well as a hefty tow bill.

It's a bugger Roy never finished that Mechanics Apprenticeship

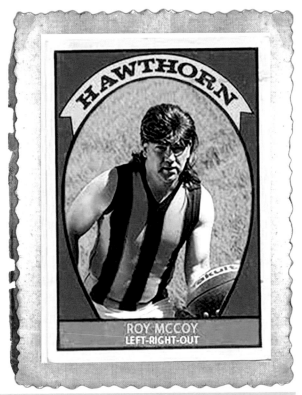

ROY MCCOY
LEFT-RIGHT-OUT

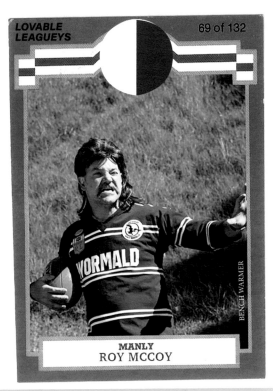

MANLY
ROY MCCOY

You can't argue he is the greatest to ever miss a granny due to car trouble

NATURAL. FEARLESS. AGGRESSIVE.
A team mate on Roy's approach to drinking

After a big night drowning his sorrows, he didn't fail to miss his flight to Sydney the next morning though. Finally donning the jersey for his beloved **Manly-Warringah Sea Eagles** after arriving at half-time, Roy came onto the ground to hear the final whistle and the sight of Sterlo and his mates raising the **Winfield Cup** for the **Parramatta Eels**.

RUGBY LEAGUE

If ET was Rugby League's pin-up boy in the 80's, Roy was right there with him. Men wanted to be him, ladies wanted to be with him... and that mullet was luscious

Roy always said sleep is as important as training in making sure you're ready to go. Here he is living by his motto on the bench during the '83 Grand Final

Roy and Dick Johnson in happier times

A fact seldom known, is in that same year he partnered guest driver **Dick Johnson**, in the very first **Targa Tasmania Rally** of '83, nine years prior to the race becoming an annual event in '92.

Roy mistakenly sent Dick left instead of right and into a ditch on the final corner, possibly the reason for it's nine year respite. Roy revealed to Dick afterwards he'd always had trouble with his lefts and rights.

Roy also helped Tasmania to fourth in the **82/83 Sheffield Shield**, averaging a very commendable 15.7 seconds from boundary to popping crease carrying two drink bottles, a fresh pair of batting gloves and the Captain's declaration intentions.

Roy's Tassie Cricket baggy green. They were kind enough to give him one even though it says TAS. XI

However it wasn't until Alan Bond and John Bertrand wooed Roy back to his love of sailing that same year that the road to stardom if not already well under construction, was certainly now paved for Roy. Bond had unsuccessfully challenged three times before for the **America's Cup – The Winfield Cup** of the sailing world, but after assembling a dynamite crew spearheaded by Roy, he returned in 1983 with a golden wrench which he claimed would be used to "unbolt the cup from its plinth", so he could take it home. And that they did, with **Roy falling overboard a record nine times during the seven race series,** even once during line crossing celebrations, forcing him to swim back to shore to join the crew for more stable on-land festivities.

"Just a bunch of Aussie legends on a boat.
Get it up ya America, the Cup's ours."
Roy McCoy speaking of the moment Australia II brought home the 1983 America's Cup - Barry & Roy are in there somewhere

Roy's unbelievable bumper year was honoured at the **'84 Australia Day** awards where he received the **Prime Minister's Most Improved.**

After hanging up the boots, bat (drink bottle), steering wheel (topographic map) and spinnaker (life jacket), Roy turned his attention to his new passion of **fishing**, and it was love at first bite. With the aid of friend and expert Barry Jeffreys, he has become one of Australia's most esteemed celebrity fisherman, mirroring his previous accomplishments (hits and misses) with unbelievable skill (enthusiasm), precision (luck) and dedication (attendance) with all he undertakes.

Roy's profile has come under scrutiny over the years, especially when his famous and much publicised rivalry with Australian icon and fellow celebrity fisherman **Rex Hunt** came to a head in the infamous Fishgate scandal (p80), but it didn't stop **Tassie's favourite son*** receiving

Roy & Rex Hunts famous rivalry dates back a long time. Roy maintains he was the first to kiss the fish before throwing it back... something that later became Hunt's signature move

the **Golden W.A.N.C.A.** (p23), the prestigious **World Association of No-Longer Competing Athletes Award** 7 years on the trot. He remains a fierce competitor and contributor to Australian sport, and in particular

*Estimation at time of print. Definitely top 5, amongst other legends Ricky Ponting, David Boon, Brant Webb and Todd Russell.

Baz & Roy were the heart and soul of the Australia II crew, and didn't they know how to celebrate.
This one was taken moments before Roy fell into the drink... again

It turns out Roy wasn't a bad open water swimmer. He did miss the first few on-shore celebratory frothies... but he made up for it

The Tasmanian Team of the Century.
Roy assures us he's in there somewhere

You know you've made it when Neale Daniher calls and asks if you wanna go down the slide at the "Big Freeze at the G" for charity. *Big Freeze II, 2016*

Roy getting pushed by Lingy & Watto (Shane Watson). *He reckons he didn't do any push-ups before hand...*

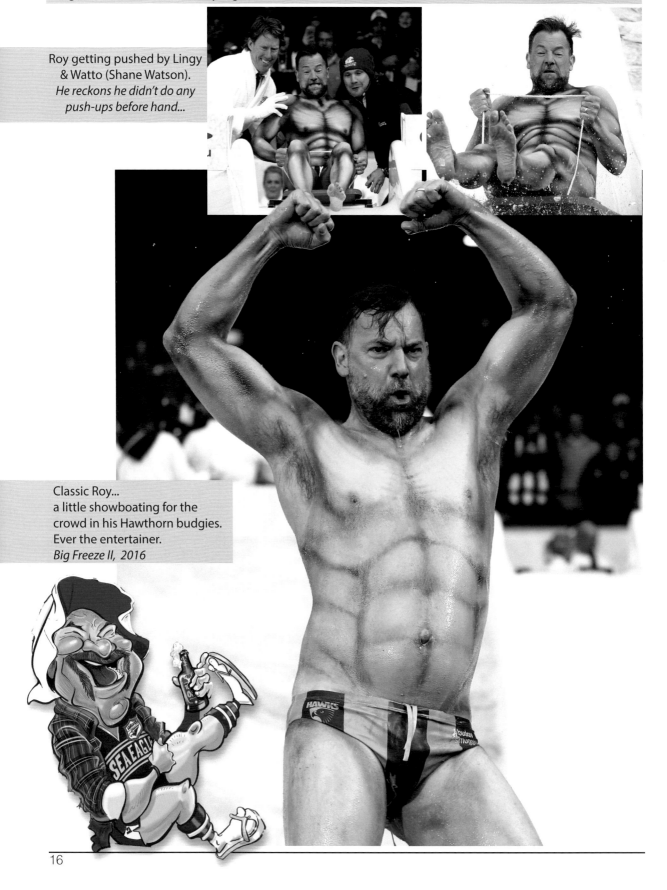

Classic Roy...
a little showboating for the crowd in his Hawthorn budgies.
Ever the entertainer.
Big Freeze II, 2016

BARRY & ROY'S ADVENTURES

AMERICA'S CUP 1983

Our fearless leader - Skipper John Bertrand and Bondy
receiving the cup. Barry & Roy just out of shot...
America's Cup, 1983, presentation

When the Skipper says go formal...
you go formal.
America's Cup, 1983

Baz making sure Roy gets full value
out of the all you can drink package
at the presentation.
America's Cup, 1983

MORE
ADVENTURES

You can get it reelin' in a marlin, or romancin' the darlin...
Matter of fact I got it now.
Baz and I enjoying a little post outing Vitamin B

Pre-1983 Grand Final as rivals.
35 years on in 2018 Roy and Barry pose with the cup again...
the rivaly is as vicious as ever.
The same can't be said about Roy's mullet

Just a couple of Premiership players... & Roy
taking in a game of AFL at the "G".
*Left to right: Roy, Barry & Chris Daniher,
MCG, Queen's Birthday, 2017*

MICK YANG

*- born... uncertain, he believes it was
between 1897 and 1911 -*

Mick Yang is what you might call a very **balanced person**. A Doctor of Philosophy and specialist in the disciplines of **Wong Kei** and **I'Stan Don Wunweg**, Mick is a spiritual consultant to the **Dalai Lama** in times of distress. A proud 3rd generation Mongolian, he personally devised the concepts of **Karma** and **Zen** and the history books show the great philosophy of perfect balance and restoration of equilibrium, Yin and Yang, was aptly named after his great great great grandfather **Yin**.

Mick is revered as a god around the world for his contribution to sporting and **fishing psychology**, working with some of the world's finest fisherman and sportsmen on becoming one with their inner-self. He has advised many great persons over his lifetime including US President Donald Trump, who actually refused to take Yang's advice. Yang now refuses to be within 10 miles of President Trump for fear of karma biting back. He also worked with Australia's long jump hero **'Jumping' Jai Taurima**, who famously claimed silver at the **2000 Olympics** in Sydney, proving a mind in touch with its spiritual core can overcome atypical lifestyle habits.

Jumping Jai locked in an intense mid-air Tai Chi pose while his high performance coach Mick Yang looks on at the 2000 Sydney Olympics

RENO GRIGIO

- born 1972 -

> *"In the spirit of exquisite dining, if it doesn't go with wine, then don't eat it"*
>
> *- Reno Grigio*

Following the emerging trend of celebrity chefs to indulge in a *little underpaying* of staff, our resident world class chef and self professed wino Reno Grigio, takes time away from his latest stint of **community service** to give all the 'foodies' a few tips on turning your catch into a culinary delight.

Reno of course was made famous after he turned the Barossa Correctional Centre's kitchen into a 5 star restaurant. He went on to produce hit TV cooking show *'If You Can't Stand the Heat, Than Get Out of The Kitchen'*, in which the theme song *'Red Red Wine'* went onto find great success. He authored the best selling *'How to Complement the Vino'* book series, the barman's bible *'Doin Time Add A Slice of Lime'* in addition to his cell classic, *'Fine Dining on a Prison budget'.*

Reno, along with a handful of other chefs, pioneered the science of **Chefridology** (Chapter 17) p.97. This radical breakthrough method involves *studying the eye of the animal* to tailor the best methods of preparing, flavouring, cooking, serving and presenting a fish.

THANK YOU'S

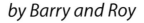

by Barry and Roy

A big thankyou to the celebrity fishing community of which Barry and I are an integral part, and of course all of our fans.

I'd like to thank that very old man who was ambling lost and dehydrated on my family's farm all those years ago, who discovered I possessed an extraordinary casting ability, for introducing me to the world of fishing. Thanks to my beautiful wife for granting me the freedom to do what I love, fish, and for bearing our thirteen kids, cos' that meant I had to get a bigger boat!

Barry Jeffrey

I'd like to thank my wife for cooking my catches. It's such a shame she's allergic to seafood. Also thanks to my boys Troy and Roy Jnr, for helping me dig out the 4WD when we got bogged on the weekend.

Roy McCoy

Roy and Barry

CHAPTER 1

The WHO'S WHO of FISHING

The Awards, Honour Rolls and photos of us with a few legends

THE WORLD ASSOCIATION OF NO-LONGER COMPETING ATHLETES AND SPORTSMEN

The **W.A.N.C.A.S** is an honour society for the aging elite. It recognises those who were once at the **pinnacle** of their sporting profession, but have since been in the public eye for reasons often unrelated to their sporting success.

More famous members have included a former multiple Tour de France winner, golfing legend and big jungle cat, a 1986 arm waving FIFA World Cup winner, a baseball bat wielding ice-skating champion, heavy weight boxing champion with a taste for ears, former Aussie Rules player with a taste for their team-mates wives, ex-Rugby League players come boxers, gambling cricketers... and footballers, Rugby Leagues 'The Bubbler', and Warwick Todd to name a few.

The W.A.N.C.A.S are recognised as they have been idolised by kids around the globe, and it is their W.A.N.C.A. - isms which so many youths wish to emulate. Of course Roy McCoy is a prize member, and has received the **Golden W.A.N.C.A a record seven times.**

The prestigious **Golden W.A.N.C.A** trophy. Roy has 7 of these life size beauties on the mantle piece making him the most distinguished W.A.N.C.A.

THE AUSTRALIAN ASSOCIATION OF EX-SPORTSMEN TURNED CELEBRITY FISHERMEN

The **AAESTCF** is the who's who of Australian Ex-Sportsmen Turned Celebrity Fishermen.

The **AAESTCF** current rankings:

1. Andrew Ettingshausen (ET)
2. Rex Hunt
3. Barry Jeffreys
4. Andrew Symonds
5. Roy McCoy

Recent inductions into the AAESTCF:
   Andrew Symonds and **Matthew Hayden** were the most notable inductions following their retirements from international cricket. Simmo was an automatic selection after showing his loyalty to fishing several times during his career. Haydo, pretty handy on the tongs after hanging up the bat, quickly climbed the rankings of the **Australian Association of Ex-Sportsmen Turned Celebrity Chefs (AAESTCC).**

Honourary award for contribution to the world of celebrity outdoors:
   Russell Coyte.

Honourary award for International Ex-Sportsman come fisherman:
   Ian Botham.

The **AAESTCF Talent ID Program** has seen future members start to work in the field of celebrity fishing in preparation for life after sport. Aussie Rules superstar **Patrick Dangerfield** (Geelong) has become a standout and even hosts his own radio fishing show, while the boys at North Melbourne have formed **The Arden Street Anglers. Mark LeCras** (West Coast and son of a fisherman) is another notable name to have been touted, with Canberra Raiders' five-eighth **Jack Wighton** a possible name to take the mantle from leagues former pin-up boy ET in life after footy.

What a hoot!
It's not everyday a couple of International Cricketers get to hangout with a couple of Celebrity Fishermen like us. It was nice of us to let them hold the fish in the photo and great of the boys to skip training to join us.
L to R: Barry, Andrew 'Roy' Symonds,
Matthew 'Haydos' Hayden and Roy (McCoy)

Dick did forgive Roy years later and they decided to go on a fishing trip together.
The terms - Roy couldn't drive the boat or navigate
(see Roy's intro for the full story, pg 14)
Dick Johnson and Roy, Circa 1994

Remember... size isn't everything.
Our squid was delicious... their lobster looked a bit rubbery.
Roy (Symonds) and Haydos and
Baz & Roy (McCoy), circa 2009

Even Barry admitted it was hard to concentrate working with *ET* - *"He's just so good looking".* *ET and Barry on set during filming of ET's fishing show circa 2003*

'Roy didn't want me to put this photo in the book but I convinced him too. It was a time when Roy and Rex could sit by a river together in harmony. Long before the Fishgate Scandal...' - *Barry*

Roy and Rex Hunt, 1998
Read about the Fishgate Scandal in Chapter 12 p80

GOT HIM!!!!! This is a great day for Australia, this is a great day for Victoria. Merv returned good figures this day with a classic spell of intimidating reeling.

Merv Hughes and Barry, circa 2006

Merv might've pipped me at the post on the squid, but surely I had him in the mo department! Just a couple of Aussie icons catching some squid...

Rex and I on the other hand always got on like a house on fire. What's not to like... he's a legend and has impeccable taste in fishing attire - *Barry*

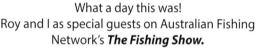

What a day this was!
Roy and I as special guests on Australian Fishing Network's **The Fishing Show.**

Here we are with host and great fella Bill Classon.
Bill tells us we got the record for ratings on 7Mate

This is a sight you don't see...
our great mate and lover of fishing
Danny 'The Green Machine' Green on the canvas!
Roy tells me they were sparring but he can't fool me.
Greeny's just giving a little scale to that beast
for the photo - Barry

The boys down at North Melbourne Footy Club have got a little fishing gang going called the **Arden St Anglers** (@ardenstreetanglers)! So Baz & I, being the forefathers of the Celebrity Fishing world, thought we had better perform our duty and show 'em a thing or two

Here's a few pics with some of the lads
from some recent adventures...
AFL ball magnet Ben 'Cunners' Cunnington
pioneering the sushi pie (above) - was a fun day!
Captain Jack Ziebell and young gun Jy Simpkin
handled themself beautifully for a couple of up and
comers (below), while Jed Anderson and Cunners
snagged a couple of lovely Tuna under the watchful
(and perhaps a little envious) eye of Roy (bottom)

Roy: Our great mate Bergy (Mark Berg) & I reeling in the big ones during filming of his show. Not your classic 'Ex-Sportsman Turned Celebrity Fisherman', but he's found his way into the club on grounds of being a cracker bloke... and not a bad fisherman either

Life on the otherside of the camera
Celebrity fishing is not all rainbows and unicorns, it can take hours to get the right expression on the squids face

CHAPTER 2

OVERVIEW and HISTORY of FISHING

This book is setup as a manual to punters everywhere. It has some very handy hints on the different techniques explored by the novice right though to the expert. It also has some good tips about fishing.

Look out for the fact file, terminology, handy hint or yarn icons, which make the book educational and entertaining for all.

KEY

 Reno Grigio shows us what he considers culinary delights, well at least what goes best with a bottle of plonk using his International 3-bottle rating system.

 STORY TIME

 TERMINOLOGY

 FACT FILE

 QUOTE

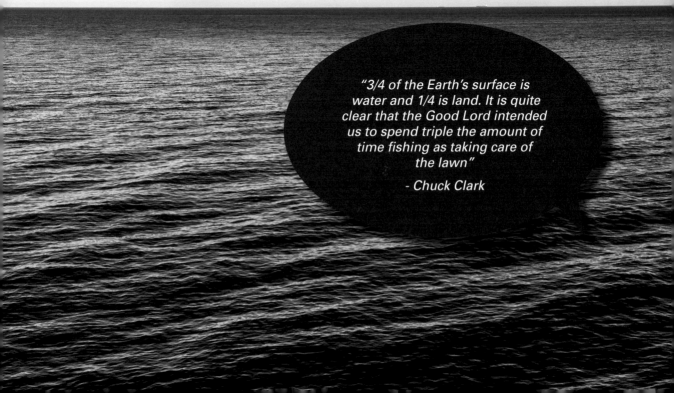

"3/4 of the Earth's surface is water and 1/4 is land. It is quite clear that the Good Lord intended us to spend triple the amount of time fishing as taking care of the lawn"

- Chuck Clark

WHO doesn't LIKE FISHING'
ACTION, RELAXATION
STORY-TELLING
MALE BONDING
and the OPPORTUNITY
TO SNEAK in SOME o
THE OLD AMBER
COLOURED WATER
FREE from UNWANTE
DISTRACTION,
ALL
LEAD TO FISHING
BEING THE SINGLE
GREATEST
ACTIVITY MAN
KNOWN TO

THE AGE OLDE DEBATE
ANGLIN' VS DANGLIN'

Both developed around the same time, each method lends itself to a differing type of fisherman.

An·glin'
Function: verb
Date: 15th century
Pronunciation: \'an-glin\

The action of one who angles; especially: the action or sport of fishing with hook and line with forceful exuberance: actively willing fish onto your line.

Dan·glin'
Function: verb
Date: 15th century
Pronunciation: \d'an-glin\

The passive act of using a hook and line to catch fish with minimal action or provocative behaviour: namely associated with such methods as the ***sit and wait method.***

Common traits of Anglers and Danglers
with Barry Jeffreys

Anglers tend to be impatient, irrational and over-energetic people. A trait is constantly checking the line, thinking they have a fish on the line when they don't and being over emotional about the entire experience.

Danglers tend to be your more content, passive, cool, calm and collected characters. Or, as Roy sees it, those not hungry enough for success, and who possess no killer instinct.

There is jovial rivalry between anglers and danglers, and you may possibly exhibit both traits. Most often what occurs is fisherman start the day as anglers and slowly but surely begin to pick up the traits of a dangler as the day wears on.

> "Dad reckons fishing is 10% brains and 95% muscle, the rest is just good luck"
> - Dale Kerrigan

Anglin' requires energy, enthusiasm... and lots of flannel

> I got caught danglin' once. The judge didn't appreciate me danglin' in public, suggested I stick to anglin'.
> - Roy McCoy

Barry... the ultimate dangler. Look at him in action

THE HISTORY OF FISHERMAN & SHARKERMAN
- THE GREAT RIFT -

Traditionally there was no such thing as a **Sharkerman.** We all came under the one umbrella – **Fishermen.** However this all changed in the late 1960's when a boat load of fishermen returning from a day out at sea declared themselves 'Sharkermen' after only catching sharks all day. Sparking debate & causing much amusement in the community, the so called 'Sharkermen' continued their practices, only targeting & catching sharks. Any fish caught by them were tragically being left on the wharf to rot as a statement to fishermen who were considered by them as lesser than their equal as hunters and gatherers. The 'sharkermen' as they called themselves, referred to fishing as 'the diet coke of sharking'.

To the shock and horror of fishermen, this new brand of seamen was spreading into the cracks and crevices of the map, with sharkermen becoming prolific around the country. Tension mounted as the alienation of these two former colleagues grew, sharkermen now electing different watering holes to share their stories after a day at sea.

Tragically the divide grew greater in 1976 when a group of disembarking and disgruntled sharkermen, who had just returned from an unsuccessful day at sea, gate crashed **The Annual Anglers and Danglers Ball**, held in The Fishermen's Lounge at Eden, NSW. It was later revealed in the Police investigation that one of the organisers of the event was the wife of a sharkerman and had cheekily ensured the menu was a selection of shark meat and the guest speaker was none other than the Great White Shark himself **Mr Greg Norman.**

As imagined this went down like a 20 pound sinker within the fishing community, and hence sparked the tension of the late 70's at ports across the country, culminating in the infamous **'Battle of the Seas'** riots of '81 on the dock at Yorkey's Knob, in north Queensland leaving 7 dead, one being gaffed after being thrown into the water.

Of course during this time, ashamedly our historians also report that many boats which disappeared off the coastlines of Australia had suffered intended ill fate, and were in fact the target of smaller radical groups, local affiliates of the sharkermen and fishermen gangs whom would sabotage the operations of others. Old folk tales reveal that spells were cast onto boats of rival companies also.

Thankfully government intervention occurred in October of 1982 and a peace agreement was reached, with every registered boat owner in the country having to pen a signature on the treaty.

With peace now in our waters, fishermen and sharkermen returned to business, and whilst there is always going to be certain tension and animosity between the two, just like any rival footy clubs, they have cast this aside for the greater focus… that big catch!!

A characature from The Brisbane Mail making light of the scenes witnessed on the dock at Yorkey's Knob, North QLD, in the 'Battle of the Seas' riot. Circa 1981

FACT FILES:

In a survey taken of attractive women, 9 out of 10 said they would prefer to date a fisherman over a doctor, lawyer, footballer & rock star, with sharkerman coming in at 27th

THE SOCIAL ASPECTS OF FISHING - THE WAGER

The most common bets placed between Anglers and Danglers are; **Who will catch the first fish, Who will catch the most fish and Who will catch the biggest fish**. Be sure that everyone on the boat is aware of the bets, the rules, penalties and of course, what they may be liable for should they lose.

Bets range from anything to a milkshake upon disembarkation at the nearest milk bar through to the pink slip of the boat (rarely seen amongst friendly anglers and danglers in the modern era, but common between fishermen and sharkermen in the 70's).

Storytime with Uncle BARRY

"On a recent fishing expedition, I made the rookie mistake of claiming the first catch and the double malted vanilla milkshake as I reeled in a 90cm Bronze Whaler Shark, only to have this overturned after a successful protest was lodged. The technicality being, the bet was for the first fish, not shark. And being in the company of devout fishermen, all wearing tight short shorts and bucket hats, who was I to argue. I was lucky I wasn't thrown overboard and gaffed for merely catching the shark".

Another one from the archives with Roy McCoy:

I'll never forget my 21st birthday. We were on a footy trip up in Wollongong and the boys all pitched in for my present and chartered a boat so we could hit the high seas and show off our hunting skills to a few local girls who got entangled with us the night before. After what one might rate as a large evening celebrating the significant milestone that is becoming the age of 21, I was woken not long after I got to bed at 5am to a great surprise; another beer, a call to get out of bed and an order to get on the boat as we arrived at the dock. Having no idea what I had myself in for, I respected the wishes of the boys and foolishly agreed to the **days wager**, having fancied myself quite the fisherman, that anyone to come home empty handed had to **stand naked on the bow** as we entered Wollongong Harbour upon return.

After a brilliant day in the sun, with only 4 of the 13 on the boat keeping the night before down, it came down to two unlucky fisherman who hadn't played a part in the mass takings which would become the nights feast, Big 'J-Lo' Jason and yours truly – the birthday boy.

With another of the boys finding luck late in what became known as **the window of opportunity** – the two minutes after delivering burley overboard when you felt good enough to once again do some anglin', J-Lo, the resident prop footballer and self-proclaimed funnyman and I found ourselves facing the humiliation of a good public pantsing coming into the harbour.

As the Captain called **lines-up** the tension rose, the sledging began and the last ditch efforts to land a catch were being brought to an end. There was a mild relief knowing both of us were in the same boat (pardon the pun), but the fact remained the todger was gonna be on full display very shortly.

Then… tragedy struck. A roaring burst of excitement from the bow, a hearty call of 'you little beauty' and the **lines up method** was born. J-Lo had indeed jagged a Sweep Fish of legal size on the final reeling in of the day to leave the birthday boy without a catch, and a debt of nudity. This was indeed honoured, bearing nothing but a fish, used in a manner reminiscent of a fig leaf by more primitive primates as we came into Wollongong Harbour. The crowd of innocent passers by, as well as the scores of patrons, waiters and chefs of the overlooking Harbourfront Restaurant letting out a good roar of laughter.

We sure enjoyed that feast and had a good laugh ourself, leaving memories of a day I'll never forget. Certainly one for the books!

Roy's 21st … he came out on the wrong end of this bet

Barry: Roy came out on top this day. If I was to win, he wasn't allowed to wear that bloody Hawthorn shirt again

CHAPTER 3

PREPARATION

"Don't worry if plan A fails... there are plenty more letters in the alphabet"

- Barry Jeffreys

WHAT TO WEAR ?

Tight short shorts are a must for any fisherman. Local authorities will check this and measure the size to ensure they comply with local regulations. Remember there are harsh penalties for not abiding by fishing laws. These must be accompanied by either a singlet, Hawaiian shirt, flanno/safari or shirt bearing a quip or quote from a previous trip or adventure.

The correct headwear is a bucket hat or 'terry toweling' which is well fitted to withstand the wind. You don't want to be the idiot who loses their hat forcing the boat to turn around giving possible cause for nomination as the **Lunch Lady** (see Terminology on across page). Note: *Corks are optional.*

We only just met local regulations this day... bit long those shorts

It's always a good idea to throw an extra one of the above mentioned in the boat per person just in case you have an unknowing rookie and are questioned by authorities. Also worth noting is the difference in dress code between fishermen and sharkermen. Please refer to the **Idiot's Guide to Sharking** for the correct sharking apparel. But remember, you're either a fisherman, or a sharkerman, don't confuse the two.

T: THE LUNCH LADY:

The famed awarding of the Lunch Lady usually comes about mid-morning, when a few stomachs start grumbling. The lunch lady is chosen by the Captain, and is the one who must leave their fishing post to prepare the lunches for the crew. It is awarded to the person who has done, said or acted in the most stupid way, or simply to someone who isn't overly well liked.

It is at the Captain's discretion who receives the dis-honours, and it must be respected. In the rare event of a successful and hiccup free morning, it will go to the youngest crewmember by default.

Gandolfe Monday-Friday...

and on the weekend. He gets it

 **FACT FILES:**

A study by the University of Bonnie Doon showed fish are more likely to go for a line of a fisherman with facial hair. Consider this when planning a trip, and maybe... leave the razor at home.

STORY OF THE FISHNETS

A yarn from Barry Jeffreys...

One of my favourite Roy McCoy moments was on his first ever *adventure on the sea,* a day that proved not only entertaining, but significant. It was a pivotal moment in his life, and the introduction to what is now a long and illustrious relationship with the recreation we know as fishing.

Roy had asked if there was anything that he could bring on the trip. I promptly replied *"a fish net"* as my previous net had been broken on its last outing. As we reached the reef, approximately two nautical miles out to sea, I asked if he'd remembered to bring it. Dropping his pants to reveal a pair of *fishnets* (firmly wrapped around his pins), the crew burst into laughter and didn't cease until returning to shore that afternoon.

Needless to say, *Roy "Fishnet' McCoy* has never lived that down and as a token of appreciation for his efforts all guests came to his surprise 40th birthday celebration in nothing but fishnets and bucket hats.

Barry: Who could forget the fishnets!

WHAT TO BRING?

BEER: Just as a marathon runner needs to replace lost fluids, a fisherman must remain *hydrated*. It's also handy to get the old war stories of fishing trips gone by flowing and emphasises that fishing isn't just about catching fish.

Beer also plays a significant part in achieving one's inner harmony (as discussed in the *Psychology of Fishing* section), and is believed to play a significant part in luring fish. Make sure the esky is *full of ice* to ensure the beer is kept at optimum temperature to maximise a *fisherman's state of mind excellence.*

FACT FILES:

Studies have shown a fisherman's story telling ability dramatically *increases* with each beer, along with the size of fish and *attractiveness of women* featured in any story. Remember when telling a story; it's your story, tell it how you want to!

ADEQUATE READING MATERIAL: It is suggested that a selection of sports magazines, *picture magazines* specific for the education of younger crew, the Trading Post and maybe the days paper be thrown in the fishing kit. A must is *The Idiots Guide to Anglin' & Danglin',* which is more of a guide to life if we're being completely honest!

SWISS ARMY KNIFE with all 45 functions

Such is the philosophy of the Swiss Army Knife inventors, you never know when you may need a mini chainsaw, saxophone, 3 in 1 eating utensil, or spare hook. Note: known as *'Army Knife'* in Switzerland.

Entry level model
Swiss Army knife

This guy knows how to test a rod.
Note bicep curls are optional

RODS: The most important feature of a rod is its bend-ability. The serious angler will make sure it can double back on itself, ensuring for great photos even without a fish in tow.

CHAPTER 4

BAIT &
non-bait
FISHING
techniques

BAIT AND HOOK METHOD

This unorthodox approach has become popular in modern times, mainly due to the commercial interests and profitability for product manufacturers. Not the most creative means of catching a fish, and not the authors' preferred method, but can be effective if done correctly. Basically as the name suggests, it involves baiting your hook, and letting it fly.

The commercialism of fishing has seen mundane methods of catching fish become the norm. BORING!

BAITING YOUR HOOK

The key to baiting your hook is to make it look appetising to the fish. Just think how you like to see your food presented and served to you.

A garnish is always a good idea, maybe a parsley leaf or curled leek shavings. Tropical fish tend to have a sweet tooth, so when fishing in warmer waters try a wedge of pineapple with an umbrella.

How could you say no to this little set-up?

BURLEY:

Commonly used by male species to attract females. A male will spray the sacred juice prior to embarking on an outing in hope that a suitable female will pick up on their scent and be hooked on the smell. Big in Europe, pioneers of this technique included Jean-Paul, Hugo 'The Boss' and Ralf Lauren.

BAIT

For those who choose to bait, the choice of bait you use is important for nailing your catch. Successful fishermen learn to be resourceful and use their environment to best match their preys' taste buds. We tend to go for road-kill, left-overs from dinner or even a lovely dessert like Grandma's apple pie. If these aren't readily available, you *can* use live bait or purchase bait from your nearest fishing shop. Boring!

> *"Good things come to those who bait"*
> - Unknown fisherman and devout user of bait

Roy picked up some bait on his way to fishing. Most people prefer to store theirs in the esky

A local hotspot for grabbing bait round the corner from Barry's...

I'd go for this if I were a fish. Try a dollop of cream to really entice the little buggers

... or if you're really stuck, try this

THE TOE-PULL METHOD

A passive fishing method used by Danglers, featuring nothing more than baited line, a few tinnies, and an afternoon nap soaking up the sun. No wonder the Danglers motto is *'A watched pot never boils'.*

Roy: An experienced fisherman like Barry can feel even the slightest of nibbles

SIT 'n' WAIT

Similar to the toe-pull, the sit 'n' wait is for the leisurely fisherman and is a danglers delight. Let the fish come to you and enjoy your day on the water.

Barry: Fishing on a hot summers day is most enjoyable, but bites can be slow to come. Often a fisherman will drink many beers before getting a single bite, like Roy here

DRAG 'n' SNAG

Some regard it lucky, but real fisherman know the truth… calculated precision. This move is the epitome of the skilful hunter and requires careful planning and knowledge of the creature you are targeting. The expert will carefully stalk its prey, learning its movements before implementing the attack.

The attack involves dropping your hook to the correct depth in the line of the traveling fish and as the name suggests dragging it along its path in order to get the hook, or 'snag' unbeknownst the fish.

T: TRENCHING:

Trenching is a technique of surveying the ocean floor to identify a trench or channel in which fish are likely to congregate. This particularly elaborate method is used before employing the **Drag 'n Snag** method to gauge what depth the fisherman's hook will need to be for greatest effectiveness. A **Depth Finder** is used to accurately measure the depth of the trench.

One of the most skillful techniques employed by fishermen is trenching. Note: authorities do random checks to ensure minimum length requirements are met

CORRECT DEPTH

This fish is about to become the victim of a textbook Drag n' Snag execution

DEPTH FINDER:

A depth finder is a very long pole used by **oceanographers** in mapping the ocean floor. It is extended and placed overboard to allow captains and fisherman alike to gauge the oceans depth. The serious angler will keep a depth finder on board. It is believed military and commercial organisations are currently working on methods of doing the same tasks using new technology known as **RADAR and SONAR**.

Many oceanographers doubt this technology will be able to match the precision of a depth finder.

NON-BAITING METHOD

The Depth Finder 3000

DROP ANCHOR:

This age old method involves timing, coordination and a big weight. It is best to **'drop anchor'** using two people, a 'spotter' and a 'spearer'. Simply put, line up the fish, and let it rip.

Try and be subtle, as you don't want to make the fish aware of the anchor coming its way. It is best to aim slightly in-front of the fish as that way it will **'swim onto it'**. Remember you want to hit the head to ensure a knock-out.

Over there!

A classic Drop Anchor on target for a direct hit and a lovely dinner

The LEAN 'n' GRAB

Much like the drop anchor, this primitive non-bait technique has been skillfully employed by fishermen for centuries. Requiring timing and hand-eye co-ordination, you must be quick, especially if the sea is running.

The preferred method for *Gumboot & Logfish*, it is a cost effective way to pick yourself up a cheeky catch without even casting a line.

Roy with one of the more aggressive kind of Lean 'n Grabs you'll see

The LASSO

LASSO:

noun; a rope with a noose at one end, used especially for catching cattle... **or fish!**

Give it a go if your after Brown Long Necks, Umbrellas, or **Antiques.** Skilful, fun & Barry's favourite.

Channel your inner cowboy

T: **THE RING PULL METHOD:**

Mainly used for Yellow-Fin Tuna and Atlantic Salmon, **Johnny West** is a genius for coming up with this little puppy. Much easier than its predecessor who required a purpose made tool, now all a fisherman need do is find the ring, give it a pull and wallah, you're guaranteed a fish.

The Ring-Pull gone wrong. Bugger

BAITING FOR A DROP ANCHOR

This is simply enticing fish to the sight in order to effectively execute a drop anchor maneuver. This can be done by various methods including throwing the left overs from lunch. The best time to do it is when a crew member is feeling off and needs to deliver some burley overboard.

Roy: "A well prepped fisherman will hit the local Chinese restaurant the night before to ensure ample burley is available"

THE BIRDS NEST:

The result of a nasty tangle in the line, leaving a right old mess that generally resembles a bird's nest. A dedicated fishing father will realise the value in lost line and not let a young fisherman rest until the line is untangled and ready for use again.

Patience and concentration can save you lots of money as this father demonstrates

"*The more knots
the stronger*"

- Roy McCoy

KNOT
worth
KNOWING

GRANNY KNOT: This *'knot for all situations'* can be used on hooks, tying the shopping bags and is the initial stage in tying a shoelace.

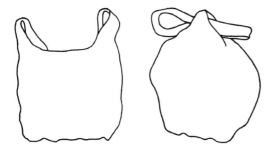

BOW: Passed down through the generations, this knot is the first one a young fisherman will usually learn & can be handy on & off the boat. Ideal for tying shoelaces and ribbon on Christmas or birthday presents and also handy in fishing, particularly for holding up your dacks.

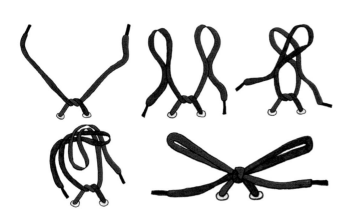

WINDSOR: Bigger fish to fry? From the board room to the high seas, this is a handy knot to know.

TRUCKIES HITCH: Originally called the *fishermans hitch*, this little beauty will keep any hook on the line. It may also be effective for keeping the boat on the trailer if a granny knot fails.

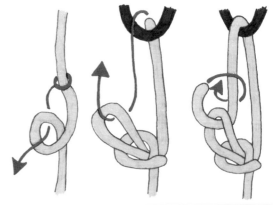

Roy's Uncle. Looks pretty happy to have mastered the hitch

NOOSE: This knot can get you out of many situations.

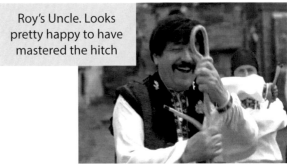

Perfect for lassoing an antique

BALLOON TIE: An ancient method, very handy when a crew member is celebrating a milestone.

THE MIXED GRILL: Basically the mixed grill is when a fisherman employs several of the knots known to him to create a combination so powerful it could give a man a heart attack.

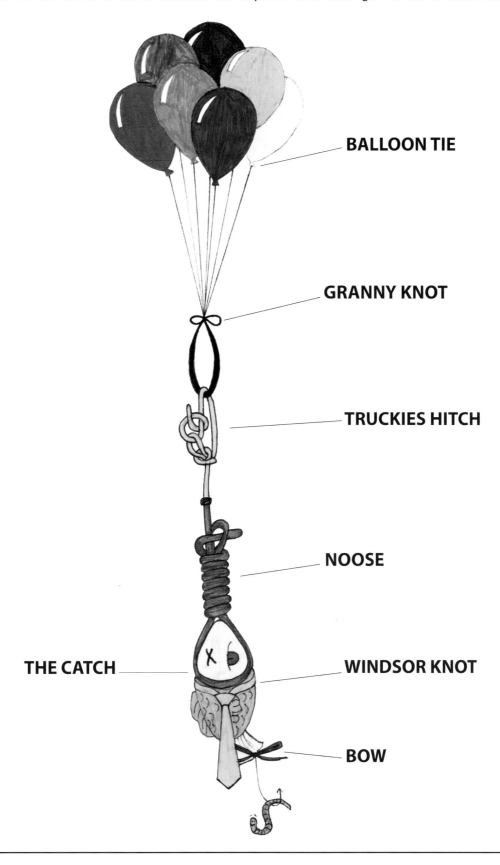

BALLOON TIE

GRANNY KNOT

TRUCKIES HITCH

NOOSE

THE CATCH

WINDSOR KNOT

BOW

WHAT YOU'LL find under the SURFACE

Species of fish & other mariney stuff

"Although between the two of us we could almost name all of the millions of marine creatures that swim below the horizon, we'd need a book that would sink your boat to fit them all. Hardly a handbook that would be!

That's why the following section is hand chosen – the crème de la crème of our personal favourites from around Australia and the globe. There are tips on *how and where* to catch them, **legal limits**, *favoured seasons* and even *tips for the* **table**. After all we don't fish for nothing. We use the common name and also show the *scientific name* for all you science-heads"

Barry and Roy

Gumboot Fish: *latex o' verfootus*

This bottom dwelling fish is more commonly found inland in dams, bays and estuaries or close to the coastline. It is found in both fresh and salt water. Like the Jagged Rockfish it can survive out of water in low tides or droughts. **Very Chewy eating**. Often served as a **cheap substitute for calamari** by some vendors because of the similar tube-like shape and texture.

Gumboot fish being sliced for the frying pan

Schnozza: *W.J. Lawryus*

Native to Victorian waters, but also caught around Australia at various times during the summer. Often travels with Chappelli's. Perfect for the Drop Anchor method as it can be spotted from quite a distance. Uncertain why, the **Schnozza** is commonly referred to as a **'Bill Lawry'**, presumably because the great Victorian and Australian opener bagged a pair in the 1973-74 season.

Got him!!! The Schnozza in all it's glory

Chapelli: *Ianolis Chappelli / Gregorius Chappelli*

Chappelli's are native to South Australia. There are **3 known species** (including the cross-bred Chappelli discussed below). The most common in Australian waters is the Ianolis Chappelli, which is known to be found with **Bill Lawry's** particularly during the warmer months. The Gregorian Chappelli has been known to be more common near the sub-continent around the waters of India over the years, but have

appeared to be back in selection in Australia. Chappelli's are known for the distinctive **orange scoop** on it's flank. Younger Chappelli's are quite sporty, and will offer resistance against any attack.

However, aging Chappelli's become boring and mundane, and are ideal for Dangler's, who may prefer to have a snooze whilst a Chappelli is **tugging your line**. There is currently a breeding program in fish farms, in which Trevally and Chappelli species are being crossbred for export to New Zealand. The fish has not been tagged a common name thus far, however it is expected that a simple combination of the species will be used such as **Trev Chappelli**. The scientific name **'underarmus bowlen.'**

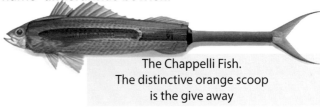

The Chappelli Fish.
The distinctive orange scoop
is the give away

Cullinan: *The Bunny*

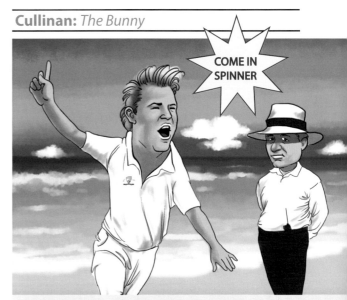

The King of Spin... the great man celebrating after jagging another Cullinane

Native to South Africa and predominant in the 90's. For such a performing fish, offering a great fight to most attacks around the world, the Cullinan proves an easy catch around Australia. If you're fair dinkum about catching Cullinan's, get down to your local and grab **Warnie's Spin Kit** and you'll be on your way. There are a lot of mind games involved when spinning. Be sure to taunt them and they'll be swimming back to the pavilion and onto your plate season after season. *If you're born after '85 - look it up.

Antique Fish: *Rich Mahogonus*

PERHAPS A GRANGE

Ideal for the Drag 'n' Snag or Lean 'n' Grab. If you spot a decent looking antique be sure to get in quick. Depending on the exact species, Antique Fish can fetch **high prices in certain markets**. Best to get an expert eye, as they say one man's treasure is another's trash.

This old waterlogged antique was caught using the lean 'n' grab technique

A recovered antique with all limbs still in place. Would fetch quite the price at market

Hippyfish: *Peecenluv*

These colourful and incredibly easygoing fish tend

Octavio Aburto

"Sweet piercing dude"

to dwell more around the waters of New South Wales northern coast, particularly the **Byron Bay** area. The Hippy is usually found feeding in waters **rich with weed**. Although Hippies are generally very chilled out, they are true lovers of their fellow fish friends and can sometimes become quite protective of them and stand up for fish's rights. If you notice a school of Hippies gathering around your boat, it's best to move to a different area to avoid their aggressive behaviour.

sabotage the murderous activities of the boat. Ironically, the Hippies were sacrificing themselves in Kamakaze missions, swimming hundreds at a time into the ship's propellor in an attempt to jam it.

A wayward photographer catches a school of angry hippies as they gather momentum before launching into the Japanese Whaling ship 'Wee Ryke Brubba'

Handy Hint:
It may be a good idea to carry a little weed on the boat, as it's medicinal qualities can aid in calming a fellow crew member in the event they become flustered

Weed: *Igot'thamuncheez*

Weed's make for a great alternative catch, with the different varieties offering a range of culinary and even medicinal options. Nori is best used in sushi, dried krill is solely used in pet fish food, whilst the cannabis sative is great smoked. Make sure you check local regulations before taking them home, or bringing aboard, as they may be protected by law and sometimes will have a bag limit. Can be an easy catch depending on the conditions... and contacts.

Hippyfish love certain weed varieties, so if you pull in some weed, there's every chance a Hippy will be nearby.

The many uses of weed

Image by stuart hampton from Pixabay

HIPPY FACT FILES:

The Japanese whaling ship 'Wee Ryke Brubba' found out about Hippies the hard way, in the most effective at-sea Green Peace demonstration to date. Fought above & below the water, schools of Hippies congregated around the vessel in a bid to

Lumberjack: *Woodchopinflannelus*

Like its Mangrove cousin, the Lumber Jack is a superb fighting and sporting, or **'working'** fish. Lumberjacks have a distinct checkered

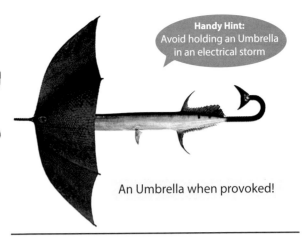

A mature Lumbarjack with a ripe beard & classic colouring

line pattern on their skin, and an abundance of long whiskers (similar to but thicker than a Catfish). The skin can range from a reddish-brown, cherry-red, to a blue with darker patches. Younger fish often show more vigour, however don't have the same power, endurance or work rate as a senior, nor the whiskers. Lumber Jacks are a tough fish with **'axe-like'** teeth. It is best to use a trace to prevent the line from being chopped.

As ambush predators, `Jacks' often dwell around mangrove roots, fallen trees, and any other areas where they may be able to snag a stray. Lumberjacks feed on logfish and will also hunt **Maid-fish** (commonly called **Barmaids**). It is commonly known the Lumber Jack **eats roots and leaves**. Because of their athletic nature, Lumber Jacks are a meaty fish, which represents great value for the table. The flesh is well nourished and abundant, particularly on a more mature Lumber Jack.

Umbrella Fish: *Brolli*

The Umbrella is what fishermen call **self-hooking**. That is, they mostly have a tail shaped as a hook, making catching them a completely new ball game. Expert fishermen will employ the Lasso method, casting just enough line to wrap the hook, reminiscent of a cowboy, before dragging it in. Umbrellas have a sixth sense for the weather and tend to show with the clouds. They have a distinct **defence mechanism** which comes out at this time of vulnerability, in which their upper body puffs into a **semi-spherical like shape** for protection, similar to that of a Frill-Neck Lizard. The bigger, more colourful variety can be caught on the beach.

A relaxed Umbrella on a clear day

> **Handy Hint:** Avoid holding an Umbrella in an electrical storm

An Umbrella when provoked!

Yellow-fin Tuna: *Tuna a la can*

Great eating fish found in brine, springwater or olive oil. Best way to catch is the **ring-pull method**.

The easiest catch you'll get. Inexpensive and even has nutritional information on it's skin

Logfish: *Eucalyptus*

This easily caught fish comes in many sizes and shapes and is most commonly spotted on or toward the surface of water. There are several non-bait techniques, which are effective for landing **Logfish** including the Drag n' Snag or the Lean n' Grab.

A couple of logs lurking dangerously in reach of would-be fishermen

Bait techniques may be effective, however if targeting Logfish, for cost-effectiveness it is better to use non-bait methods. Logfish, or **'logs'** are not a great fighting fish, nor good eating, but can make a great table fish, and also make for great trophies.

A great tablefish

The cross section of a logfish. Experts say you can tell the age by counting the rings

An old dried up riverbed where a school of Logfish onced lived. They became petrified in their later years

Logfish are more commonly spotted near land or down stream. Larger Logs may be found on the bottom of creeks and rivers. Extraordinarily, they can live to very great ages, at which times they can become distressed, or petrified if held at great depths with minimal oxygen. Although Logfish mightn't be the ideal fish for the active angler, remember **where there's Logs, there'll be Lumber Jacks.**

Clinger: *Stagus Penta*

Always found by the side of a male fish of any variety, a Clinger will pick a companion and stay very close to it. Ideal for a **double catch**. Try using 2 hooks on a drag 'n' snag, or with the lines-up. If you grab the dominant but frustrated male as he attempts to break free, you're sure to get the Clinger also.

CAUTION STAGE 5 CLINGER!

Shark covered in clingers... bit of a pimp

Silverfish: *Lepisma Saccharina*

A common pest, eaten by larger animals, it's common name is derived from the animal's silvery light grey and blue colour, combined with the fish-like appearance of its movements, while the scientific name indicates the silverfish's diet of carbohydrates such as sugar or starches. *

The best way to catch this one is the same way you caught '*Louis, that God Damned Fly.*'

*This is actually true

Close up of an adult Silverfish

Cuddlefish: *'The teddy bear of the sea'*

Great trophy fish and make for great photos. Remember to bring a few extra coins and some persistence if you're fair dinkum about catching a Cuddle. You may have to wrestle a carny if you want to get a big one.

18+

A few varieties of Cuddlefish

Brown Long Neck: *Veebee-inthesea*

Ideal for the table, but for ornamental or thirst quenching reasons. Not ideal for eating. Fresh born **Long Necks** are known to float on the surface making the lean 'n' grab or Lasso method preferable. Long Neck's retain water as they age and tend to sink embedding themselves on the lake or sea bed, often by **Dimple Fish.**

A school of older Long Necks - green and brown varieties

A youthful Brown Long Neck locked in a staring competition with a Dimple Fish

Champagne Fish: *Moet*

The ritzy cousin of the Brown Long Neck, mainly found in waters off southern France, the Champage Fish is a real fizzer!! Great with canapes and to celebrate special occasions. Beware of cheap immitations.

This diver found himself a Moet! Chin Chin

Barracuda: *The Tenpin Bowler*

Barracudas can attack with great surprise. They can be fun and a little different, but sometimes aren't well received by a partner. Although using a little charm like with a Spanish Lady is a sweet idea, plenty believe a firmer hand and a good hook is needed to jag one. A Spanish Lady - Barracuda double in one outing is very commendable amongst anglers.

Reno says this one goes down a bit easier after a few bottles

FISH FROM AROUND THE WORLD

Red Snapper: *Herschelli Gibbus*

Named after the great South African cricketer, the **Red Snapper** has been known to wriggle its way out of a catch at the last minute. This defence m e c h a n i s m sees it trick the fisherman into thinking he's got the catch, before

Remember... don't count your catch till it's firmly in your hands and on the scoreboard, you'd hate **to drop the world cup!**

kicking out at the critical moment when in hand. Spotted during the summer months, a Red Snapper can be a pain in the hind offering resistance to the attack. A quick action and keeping your line on a good length should do the trick.

Field placement is important, make sure you have a line at mid wicket

Bubba-fish: *biggus lippus*, aka 'sweet lips'

Bubba's came from the deep south of America. It is believed they were introduced to South-East Asia during the 60's, as they have been spotted in jungle streams in and around most notably Vietnam. They now survive on the high seas and are often found around **Gumpfish**. Bubba's feed on shrimp and hence are prolific in shrimp season. They are a fantastic table fish and are used in many dishes.

"Anyway, like I was sayin', fish is the fruit of the sea. You can barbecue it, boil it, broil it, bake it, saute it. Dey's uh, fish-kabobs, fish creole, fish gumbo. Pan fried, deep fried, stir-fried. There's pineapple fish, lemon fish, coconut fish, pepper fish, fish soup, fish stew, fish salad, fish and potatoes, fish burger, fish sandwich. That - that's about it."

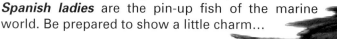

Great catch. Love to what we the experts call *'tango'* before you pull them in. They look good, taste great and are perfect with a little Sangria.
Spanish ladies are the pin-up fish of the marine world. Be prepared to show a little charm...

Sangria best

HR:138

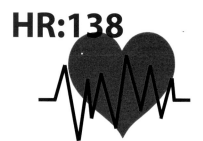

TANGO:

When a fish rhythmically moves or **'dances'** whilst on your line. Trait of fish around Latin America and Mediterranean regions and specific to Spanish Ladies.

FACT FILES:

The word *'Tango'* originated from a saying of Mediterranean fishermen. It is said, when they felt the rhythmical movements on the line, it meant a catch was imminent and they would be heading inside out of the sun to cook and eat the fish. The word literally means for ones **tan to cease; tan-go.** Of course, now the word is used to describe a style of dancing which imitates the movements felt from Spanish Ladies on your line.

CHAPTER 6

&CRUSTACEANS &EXOTICS

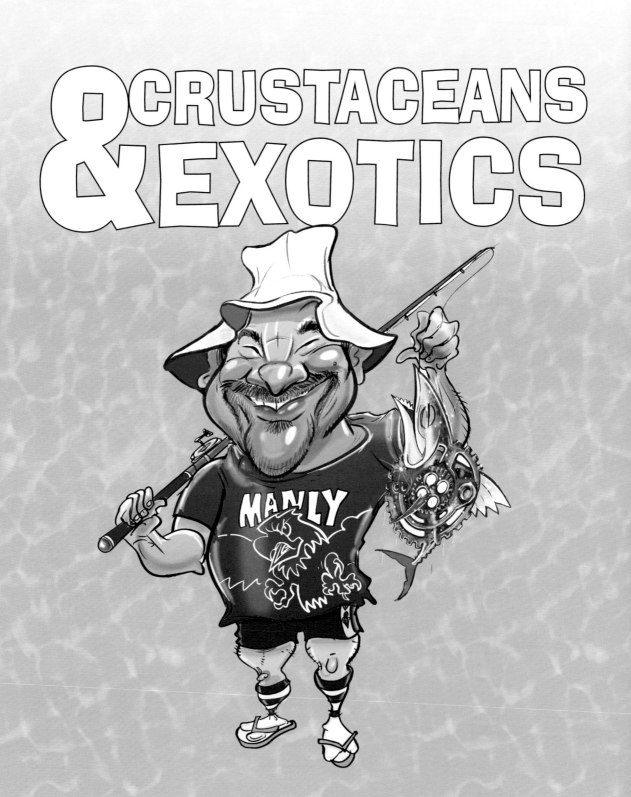

Jagged Rockfish: *Resulta Vulcanus*

Cousin to the extremely dangerous **Stonefish** (and similarly camoflauged), this bottom dwelling fish is found around reefs, headlands, shoals and islands. They are a great fighting fish and known for their strength although you won't feel a nibble before hooking this fella. They can maintain their **still position** despite your best efforts to reel them in and have provided many fisherman with the "one that got away" story. Seem to not be tempted by bait, so save yourself some pennies and stick to non-bait techniques.

Amazingly, the Jagged Rockfish can survive out of water during low tides. They are **cleverly camouflaged as a rock** and may be to sharp to pick up. Not considered a great tablefish and has no bag limit, but if you can manage to haul one into the boat, you may want to kiss him, snatch a Kodak moment & take him home for the front garden.

A Jagged Rockfish of legal size

Scorpion: *Phire-claws*

Cousin to the exquisite culinary delight the red lobster, the **Scorpion** although smaller in size is somewhat of a delicacy itself.

Found on menus and back street stalls of certain Asian countries, Scorpions have some bite of their own.

HR:
R.I.P.

Bearded Clam: *Kneedzawaksus*

The 70's saw a growing trend of Bearded Clams on menus across the world. Ideal for dining in and also eating out. Ensure it is cleaned prior to being served. Bearded Clams have died out since the 70's with them rarely spotted nowadays. The more attractive cousin 'The Brazilian Clam' or **'Brazilian'** is much more prominent now and can be found around the world.

Handy Hint:
Wash your hands before heading home

No photograph due to censoring laws

Cog: *Speen Onaxl*

There are a number of Cog species, the most common the **Atlantic Cog**. Usually found dwelling around shipwrecks, Cogs have a disc-like shape and a natural defensive mechanism, with teeth placed continually around their circumference. They are a practical fish, but become affected by seawater over time which changes their colour and often shape. **The Bermuda Triangle** is said to be flooded with Cog's.

A classic Atlantic Cog, common in the deep waters of the Bermuda Triangle! Notice the discolouration of it's teeth

Starfish: *Lazyonbakus*

They look good and are very exotic, but are they really worth it? A lot of work on your behalf, but still a catch and indeed a story at the end of the day. Besides, using the **Unwritten Code of Fishing**, its your story, tell it how you want, no one will ever know.

A classic starfish... You've gotta do all the work!

Horn-fish: *Erectus Maximus*

Alcohol may hinder the Horn's ability to activate it's defence mechanism

This little trail blazer has a defence mechanism not rivaled by many, and intimidating to others. Dominated by, and under constant harassment from females, the male reacts by erecting a sword like falice with which it plunges into the female to withstand its attack. Not recommended on the table, although some bizarre cases in Europe have seen the horn eaten. Ouch!

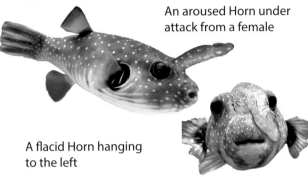

An aroused Horn under attack from a female

A flacid Horn hanging to the left

This fella got caught up in a school of Brown Long Necks, and it looks like he has a bottle by midday sort of addiction

Combining Tai Chi with catching dinner has become popular in many South-East Asian countries. The stresses of modern life means sometimes we just don't have enough hours in the day to do the things we love

Just as it's recommended to stop, revive, survive on long trips in a car, it's also a good idea to pull onto some rocks for a nap when boating

MORE
FISHING STUFF

"Arriba"

Barry: Roy will often pull a last minute surprise and declare a dress-up theme for a fishing trip. This one was Mexican day... not Coronas in hand, but they do say Victoria is Mexico

This rooster has got the 'Official Photo' hold down pat - thrust the fish towards the lens so the fish appears bigger. Apparently he writes a pretty funny fishing manual too...

Just when you thought fishing couldn't be anymore fun, your mate brings a bow & arrow!

Don't know how his six year old grandson feels about this catch... at least they found him

FLY FISHING

Roy: Although it is said...

"the best way to a fisherman's heart is through his fly"
Barry & I still don't understand why you would want to fish for flies...

ICE FISHING

> *"I wonder what the Captain of the Titanic would say?"*

Barry:

"Just like the numb minded people who fish for flies, there are those from the colder parts of this world that fish for ice. The point of the exercise…? Well that's a good question! I'd much rather grab a bag from the servo. Apparently it is quite popular in parts of Canada, Siberia, Russia and Tasmania, all particularly strange countries indeed".

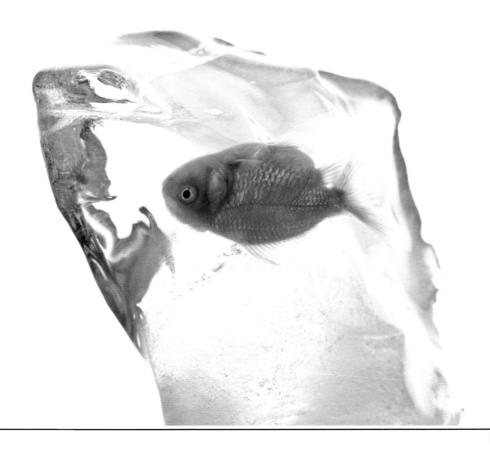

CHAPTER 9

"LOCATION
LOCATION
LOCATION"

TOP SPOTS

With Australia's vast coastline and river systems providing a plethora of fantastic fishing spots for anglers and danglers alike, its hard to narrow a favourites list down to a few... the following highlight some of the best this country, and the world has to offer.

- ○ Wolfe Creek
- ● Lake Eyre
- ◐ Bonnie Doon
- ● The Bermuda Triangle
- ◐ Kiama Blowhole

Wolfe Creek

A large round creek a short drive away from civilisation.

Note: don't trust any locals if you're car breaks down... or drink the water.

Lake Eyre

A large lake... a short drive from civilisation.
Bring the chips... and the fish.
The salt's provided.

Lake Eyre in all it's glory

Bonnie Doon

A large doon, great for carp. Picturesque and great spot for the family. Known for the theme song 'We're goin' to Bonnydoon', and of course... the serenity.

The Bermuda Triangle

A large triangle somewhere in between The America's and The Africa's. BYO survival equipment. Rich with Cog's (see Fish Species).

Kiama Blow-Hole

One of a series of blow holes around the Australian coastline where you'll see fishermen lining up for a *classic catch*. It's all about timing, hand eye co-ordination and soft hands. Similar to fishing with dynamite, the blow-hole's natural power blasts fish into the air for hustling fishermen to scramble for a mark. The blow-hole has become an integral place of training for aspiring AFL protégés, 80's hardman **Dermott Brereton** often spotted as a junior climbing the backs of on-looking tourists in search of a classic at the top of the square... ah... viewing platform.

Derm training at the Blowhole

CHAPTER 10

"My biggest worry is when I'm dead and gone, my wife will sell my fishing gear for what I said I paid for it"
Koos Brandt

BOATING

CHRISTENING THE BOAT

It can't be stated enough the importance of **christening** a boat. As discussed below, failure to christen a boat properly endangers the boat and its crew whom become susceptible to curses, voodoos and bad luck. This should be done by striking a bottle of **champagne** over the bow of the boat prior to departing on its maiden voyage (a cheap substitute such as **Passion Pop** maybe used at the owners discretion and risk).

Barry: Roy christening '**The Real McCoy I**'.
I told him he should've gone a bit more up market than **Passion Pop**, but he didn't listen.
Go to Pg. 70 for the end to this story

THE HISTORY OF BOAT CHRISTENING

As the tale goes, when a young **seaman** was commissioned with the task of bringing some liquid entertainment on a fishing expedition, he mistakenly chose a bottle of champagne. This was duly smashed over the bow of the boat by a disgusted **Captain** because it wasn't beer. The boat ended up being one of only two that survived the **Great Storm of 500 B.C.**, the other being a travelling circus skippered by a **Captain Noah**. Hence, the act was considered **good luck** and the ritual was born.

PLUGS / BUNGS

These little buggers can mean the difference between a good day on the sea, and a good day in the sea. Always remember to put the plugs in the boat (recommended before departing the port) to prevent the **fast leak effect**.

Always a good idea to throw a few extras in as spares. Plugs come in a variety of shapes and sizes depending on the bung-hole.

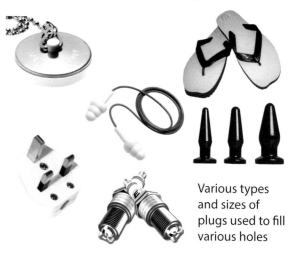

Various types and sizes of plugs used to fill various holes

T: **THE FAST LEAK EFFECT: Inflow > Outflow**

This is usually noticed too late, but is definitely worth being aware of. It occurs when the vessel **fills quickly with water**, presumably because of a structural fault in the boat or the plugs not being utilised. It is best to attempt to bucket or pump out the water while assessing the problem. If the rate of inflow of water is considerably greater than the rate of outflow, the members of the crew should consider changing into their swimming trunks and limbering up a little.

Became a victim of the fast leak effect

TIPS FOR BOATING

Puncture repair kit. A good idea to have in case you cop a flat on the road or run a ground at sea and split the hull. Patches come in various sizes.

Jump starting the boat; in much the same way as you jump start the Datsun before work, the trick here is getting some momentum up. The best way is to get on a runner & ride the wave before pulling the cord on the engine. Just be careful if you're heading towards shore as the potential for capsizing and/or beaching increases with the size of the swell and proximity to the shore.

This fella is working at 200% above Barry's recommended level of enthusiasm for a standard jump start

HANDY HINT:

Urinating aboard: As a result of tests conducted by the **Anti-Boat-Rust Institute, the industry** recognised and standardised stance is feet shoulder width apart, knees bent at 22° from the vertical, with one arm (generally the less favoured) supporting. For a circumstance in which a woman is aboard, the same applies.

Note: Heavy fines are issued by authorities if found to be in breach of this.

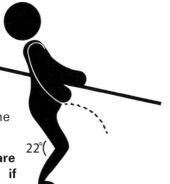

22°

SEA SICKNESS:

Sea sickness or motion sickness is a common ailment causing much angst amongst those who take on the high seas. It is caused by continual movement upsetting ones inner ear balance. Thankfully, medical researchers have developed a drug to combat sea sickness.

The drug's chemical name is **ethyl hydrate**, and works by disorienting the brain, causing its own form of internal motion, effectively cancelling out the motion sickness in what is known as the *"double negative effect".* Some researchers believe administering the drug has a placebo effect, somewhat tricking the brain into thinking it is just in a regular intoxicated state. Ethyl hydrate can be purchased in many flavours and strengths at any bottle-o.

It should be noted that a real fisherman does not suffer from sea sickness, but will always carry and administer the drug for preventative purposes

Common forms of ethyl hydrate

The three clinical stages of Sea Sickness:

Stage 1. Afraid you're going to get sick

Stage 2. Afraid you're going to die

Stage 3. Afraid you're not going to die

AN ACCIDENTAL HISTORY OF BOATING

A story about The Real McCoy...
with Barry Jeffreys

Now I'd go as far to say my mate Roy McCoy is an expert of the sea. But he's never had much luck with boats. A long list of mishaps, courtesy of a series of unfortunate events sees him on his 7th boat.

Here's the story of the Real McCoy I, II, III, IV, V and VI.

The Real McCoy I: A victim of the **fast leak effect** (see page 68) due to forgetting to put the bungs in, resulting in capsizing, and a long swim across **Moreton Bay**, QLD. Guest of Roy's that day, Duncan Armstrong, impressively set the record for the 8km swim home to raise the alarm in known Bull Shark territory.

Roy didn't help by going cheap on the christening (see page 68 - Christening the Boat).

Roy...
"If only I had paid attention a little better at Scouts..."

The Real McCoy III: Roy's pride and joy changed owners over the poker table one evening. His seemingly unbeatable off-suit hand of 2 and 8 not enough to overcome Rex Hunt's Full House.

The ol' Full House has cost many a brave punter the slips of their vessel.

Roy atop the Real McCoy I in its final moments while Duncan Armstrong swims to raise the alarm

The Real McCoy II: The fate of the second edition of the fleet came courtesy of an insufficient **Granny's Hitch**, the boat and trailer parting ways en route to the water for a days fishing.

When it comes to Roy's arch rival - Rex Hunt - he just can't help himself. Here is my ol' mate goading Rex into putting the keys on the table. You see what happened next...

The Real McCoy IV: The unique story of The Real McCoy IV saw the boat being traded in to make way for the more spacious, and practical Real McCoy V.

The Real McCoy V had a good spell until it was decommissioned due to stress fractures in the hull (possibly as a result of several incidences involving rocks).

It was the elusive missing boat of '02. After weeks of planning and researching the area for filming on Roy's celebrity fishing and adventure show - **Boy's Toys with Roy McCoy**, the gear was packed up and the crew embarked on the 9hr drive to the destination, only to realise on arrival that no one had hooked the boat on and it was still sitting in the driveway. By all reports it ended up being a good week away, the local watering hole the new hotspot for fishermen in the area.

The **ABC** was believed to be unimpressed by the ordeal, but after viewing the footage, used it in a documentary discussing the alcoholic behaviour of men on 'boys trips' away.

The Real McCoy VI:
His 6th boat, **The Real McCoy VI** is thought to be in the Tasman Sea somewhere. After a day of fishing and the opportunity for a 'quick beer' and telling of a sea yarn at the Pub on the Dock, Roy ventured back to his vessel to settle in for the night... well so he thought. Turns out he fell asleep on the deck of another boat while the Real McCoy VI was drifting out to sea with the tide.

The matter has set a precedent in the courts, with Roy still arguing the insurance policy didn't **NOT** cover such an event.

Where Roy's boat was meant to be

Where he woke up...

Barry: Even the best have an off day...
Roy forgot to top up with petrol and we would've been stuck out at the
reef had it not been for the legend Skipper from *Cairns Reef Fishing*.
Here we are down on our luck... before we found out he had a full esky!

CHAPTER 11

TIPS FOR LOOKIN' LIKE A REAL Angler FOR THE LENS

THE OFFICIAL PHOTO

t is the photo which will be framed and put on the wall to remember. Normally marking a monumental moment like a young fishermans first catch, you want to make sure the prize photo does your hard work justice, and when I say justice I mean justice with interest!

To get the most out of your photo stand flat footed clutching the fish with a sturdy grip by the tail, just below the rear fin, as seen below.

Now **thrust the fish towards the camera** maximizing the angle from lens to fish to fisherman, enhancing the size of the fish gaining up to 50% proportional to the fisherman's body size.

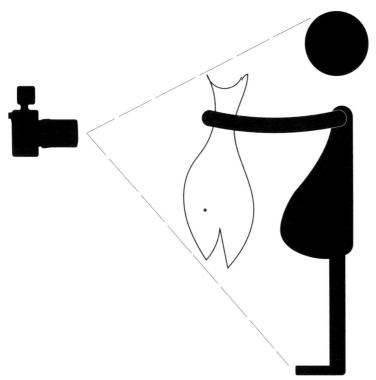

Diagram of the offical photo stance

This little fella's got the right idea, although I don't know how much it helped!

"Mate I'm telling ya, she was on. Fought her for an hour and a half. Was a biggen, I reckon at least 40kgs!"

PHOTO OF THAT CATCH:

Always be aware when a camera's around and don't be afraid to ham it up a little for the lens. For any action shots of you reeling in, ensure the rod is always **bent back on itself**. This will support any stories that come later.

Barry: A few pics from behind the scenes filming **'Boys Toys with Roy McCoy'.**
Roy is expert level when it comes to hamming it up for the cameras

Me on the other hand, I just love taking it all in....

CHAPTER 12

THE LAST RESORT

Fish outlets around Australia

THE 'LINES UP' DIDN'T WORK?

We've complied a handy list of top fresh outlets around the country so you don't go home empty handed.

The One That Got Away!
Bald Knob, NSW

One of Roy's old haunts. Great snapper. Dave will even put a hook in its mouth for you... the seal of authenticity.

Don't worry about dinner Honey.. I'm goin' Fishing!!
Halfway up the dirt track on the left, Pimpinbudgie, QLD

Very small hole in the wall market style shop only known to real anglers. Get in early. Stocks dwindle as those disembarking line-up to ensure they impress the Mrs. Handy to know - the proprietor Charlie is a retired physician, and is more than happy to help out with a Medical Certificate to show your boss, wife or mother-in-law.

Been Fishin'!
Upsndowns, VIC

This little beauty has everything from scorpion-fish to rockfish, and he'll even take a pic of you proudly holding it on the dock.

Just Fish...
Innaloo, W.A.

Great shop, great range, great location. Also does taxidermy so you can make the purchase last, cementing your legend as a classic angler for the future generations.

Fish Fish More Fish
The End of the World, TAS

In the far south there's no excuses for missing out on a fish. Best you pop in and see Bob and Bernie down at the end of the world. Guarantees absolute discretion with a no camera policy. Specialises in Brown Long Neck's, but may keep you to sample one with him before you go.

SECRET MEN'S BUSINESS

Become a member of the *'Don't go home empty handed Society'* for a comprehensive list of outlets around Australia. Be sure to look out for the *"bearded fisherman"* which signifies it's membership.

This will guarantee A grade fish, absolute discretion, and many will offer photoshopping services to mimic the catch photo on the water. If you really wanna impress the other half, you can pre-order your fish, tell 'em what you're hunting for so they can look up recipes, and deliver everytime. How good is that!

The Bearded Fisherman - the signal of a member store

Barry & I are of course **Platinum Members**, but I only use it to fool the Mrs or mates.

This has become a hot topic over the years, and one which Barry will re-tell the tale overleaf... as I have nothing to prove to anyone.

See the 'Bearded Fisherman' on the counter... & the not so subtle sign

Roy McCoy found himself in hot water over his alleged mis-use of the Last Resort. This is now known as the Fishgate scandal

FISHGATE

as told by Barry

The fishing world was rocked in 2011, when the Fishgate scandal erupted after allegations **Roy McCoy** had not actually **caught the** fish which made him the recipient of the industries top prize, **The Big Fish Award.** When Paulie Paulson, local fishmonger, seafood vendor and supposed friend of Roy's from his hometown of Eggs & Bacon Bay, Tasmania, came forward with shocking information that Roy had in fact purchased the 3.7m Sailfish which saw him take out the renowned annual nationwide fish off, from his hole in the wall outlet.

The saga made headlines world-wide, and Roy, who had long lived in the eye of greatness, had been reduced to nothing.

Roy, maintaining he was innocent, fought the public scrutiny and battled to keep his name free from further defamation.

It didn't help my good mate's cause however that no one had witnessed his **BIG FISH** being reeled in, as it was a reconnaissance trip, in which he didn't want his new hotspot to be found out by other anglers. It also didn't help that he'd dropped his phone overboard whilst trying to snap a selfie with the wrestling beast, and that the **only existing pic** of the catch was unfortunately taken on his wife's camera in the backyard of the family home.

79 year old local publican Bob Barstool, came forward to say he had seen the fish in Roy's boat as he brought it up the ramp the morning of the alleged fishing trip. His eye-witness account was dismissed however, after it was heard old Bob had finished the better half of a bottle of scotch after closing the pub at midnight, before going on to see the fish just after sun up.

The twist in the story came when it emerged Roy's long-time foe Rex Hunt had made his way to Eggs & Bacon Bay three weeks after Roy had publicly announced his catch. He reportedly visited **Paulie Paulson's** shop, just days before Paulson appeared on **A Current Affair,** going public with the **shock revelation that Roy had bought the fish from him**. Paulson of course had photos he'd taken over the years with Roy on visits to his shop after many failed fishing trips, which served as 'proof'. Hunt was seen paying for his fish & chips with a **brown paper bag**. Paulson affording to take his family – all 13 sons and daughters and 4 wives (one current and three ex's) on a long overseas holiday shortly after. Particularly odd if you ask me.

The matter is 'officially' resolved, however to this day many have come to realise that **Roy was a victim** of his own character... & bad habits. Some believe in Roy and his catch of a lifetime, some not.

The stripping of the title however, which would be awarded to next in line **Hunt**, is considered to sit amongst sports **greatest controversies**, rated second in the **'Guiness Book of Great Sporting Controversies'** to the heavily publicized ice skating soap opera fought out between the US's Nancy Kerrigan's knee and **Tonya Harding's** then boyfriends baseball bat.

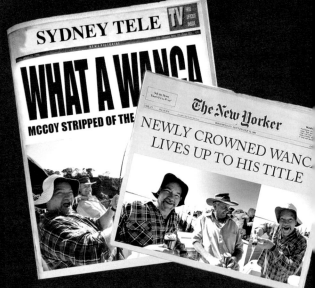

CHAPTER 13

DEALING WITH THE SIGNIFICANT OTHER

"The best way to a woman's heart is to catch her a fish"

Barry Jeffreys

"Men and fish are alike. They both get into trouble when they open their mouths"

Mrs Jeffreys

DEALING WITH THE SIGNIFICANT OTHER

Baz waves goodbye to a very understanding Mrs Jeffreys as he heads off for another fishing trip

When a significant other applies pressure about the need for yet another fishing trip, it is handy to have a few responses on-hand to smooth things over, prove to her that yes it is necessary and most importantly, ensure the nights horizontal activities are not in jeopardy.

A survey taken of expert fishermens other halves, convinced of the benefits of their husbands' fishing habits, revealed these reasons to be amongst the best:

- it provides time to prepare a lovely meal for him.

- it provides time to clean the house without getting in the way of the TV.

- it allows time to take stock of the beer fridge whilst it is not under constant changes in inventory.

- it provides your man time away from the stress of work.

- it gives him a great opportunity to discuss with fellow fisherman the ways to romantically surprise you.

- it gives him a chance to share useful knowledge and learn about things such as jewellery store locations and ring designs from other anglers.

Below is some first hand accounts of women who understand the importance of fishing, and the positive effect it has on their relationship.

"My husband told me that he is old fashioned and likes to be the hunter and provider for his wife and family. So when he embarks on his weekly fishing trip I know that he is thinking of me and is out there working hard to keep us nourished and happy. It's done wonders in the bedroom too, particularly after I agreed to let him buy a new boat."

"I would never hesitate to let my hubby go fishing with the **health benefits it provides**. No better way to stay in peak physical condition then wrestling a few fish."

"My guy is so unique and romantic. He likes to measu his love for me with fish. He mu really love me... last week he we fishing for 3 days and brough home 1 fish. Come to think of it

"Truth be told... I wouldn't mind if he went fishing a lot more. Gets the lazy sod out of the house so I can get the girls over and the bubbles flowing"

Janny D

"If that b*stard goes on one more bloody fishing trip..."

Mrs McCoy (Roy's wife)

CHAPTER 14

KNOWING YOUR FISHING ENVIRONMENT

The elements add a degree of variability to any fishing trip. It is important to turn these adverse conditions into an advantage for you and your fellow anglers.

JOHN'S
WEATHER FORECASTING STONE

CONDITION	FORECAST
Stone is Wet	Rain
Stone is Dry	Not Raining
Shadow on Ground	Sunny
White on Top	Snowing
Can't See Stone	Foggy
Swinging Stone	Windy
Stone Jumping Up & Down	Earthquake
Stone Gone	Tornado •

The Weather3000 developed by Johnny down at NASA to give precise weather conditions in real time. Also great for Anglers

Many a good days fishing has been lost due to unreliable weather forecasts, so our advice is to get out there and weather the storm. You can never rely on the weather forecast. Thunderstorms and high winds... yeah right!!

SEASONS:

The seasons play a vital part in planning a fishing trip. Obviously September is a hard time to plan a trip because of *footy finals*, and immediately after this the *cricket season* begins. The warmer weather in summer paired with cricket being ideal for radio updates, does make for better fishing.

GLOBAL WARMING AND ITS AFFECTS ON MODERN FISHING:

As water levels rise, it will certainly become easier to get the boat out of the water. In that regard, Global Warming is of benefit to fishermen. For those living in the suburbs, they will have a shorter commute before they're on the water, not to mention their now waterfront homes will most certainly fetch a higher price.

The effect of increases in water temperatures can only be viewed as positive as in the event of capsize, the water will be much more pleasant for the swim back to shore.

On many still waters, the margins may be very soft and even swampy. A solid platform will enable you to fish in safety and comfort. However, don't be concerned if you do end up in the drink. This will signal to fish that you are not a threat but wish to share the waters, even arousing their interest and drawing more to the area for fellow anglers to cash in on.
Unlike Roy here

TIDES:

Using tides to your advantage.

Getting caught out on a tide is not always a bad thing. Sure you may run aground, and be stranded until water returns up to 6 hours later. However if there are still **beers in the esky** it provides a good opportunity to get rid of these reducing the weight of the boat and also enjoy the company of fellow fisherman without the **stresses of fishing**. It also gives you a chance to further appreciate a significant other who may be waiting at home. As they say; **'absence makes the heart grow fonder'**.

The difference between the pro's and
the weekend warriors.
We know where all the dangers are...
and we have a bit more fun too!

CHAPTER 15

THE PSYCHOLOGY OF FISHING

with Barry....& Mick Yang

SUPERSTITIONS, ZEN, KARMA AND FISHING MYTHS EXPLAINED

"Near to rivers, we recognize fish, near to mountains, we recognize the songs of birds. It is very important to make on-the-spot investigations"

We spoke to Zen Master *Mick Yang* who gave his thoughts on Myths, Zen and Karma in fishing from his more than qualified point of view.

As a young boy, Mick took notes from his great great grandfather Yin Yang, and has built on Yin's work. Mick, a 3rd generation Mongo-Australian, said his Mongolian was a bit scratchy, but he's pretty sure he got it all...

"While there may be an art and even science to fishing, *Karma* is the most important element."

"Great fishermen miss out at times and rookies sometimes catch the biggest fish. All the science and art of fishing cannot overcome luck. Get your luck back by adjusting your personal *Zen*."

"Fish are not the sharpest tool in the shed. They have little more than a brain stem that takes them through life. Breeding, feeding and survival for fish is all based on primitive instincts. While some fish may learn basic things, that behaviour is due to *primitive conditioned behavior.*"

"Just like *Pavlov's dog.* To increase your odds, use your primitive brain. Be one with the fish. Use art and science to prepare for fishing, but use *Zen* when fishing."

Proper balance is important. If Yin out weighs Yang then fish sense the imbalance.

T: *Yin and Yang:* In Chinese philosophy, yin and yang (also "dark—bright") describes how opposite or contrary forces are actually complementary, interconnected, and interdependent in the natural world.

BARRY and ROY - The ACADEMICS

Roy and I recently **studied** the affect opening a fresh **beer** had on fishing performance. We noticed on quite a few occasions that fish tended to bite after we opened a fresh **beer.** Yin suggested that at this moment, your **focus** changes placing **balance** in your thoughts. He told us the thought of that *"ice cold refreshing amber* wipes your mental slant clean of impurity. This oneness with your inner self triggers universal harmony. You are one with your **inner fish."**

Roy's wife pointed out that it was likely that whenever we catch a fish it's just after we opened a beer, because *'you bloody blokes drink so much'*, but the science seems flawless.

Yin went on; "The same is true with other basic instincts. Open a dumpling, doze off or even take a leak, fish will feel the oneness with basic nature. While drinking plenty of **beer** and frequent **urination** go hand in hand to produce a fine catch, strive for the satisfaction of catching without the use of alcoholic trickery. It is not to say that you should not have **beer**. Just limit your consumption to improve your ability to maintain balance."

Of course, Roy and I don't necessarily agree with that last bit.

Average Beer-Pee-Fish Ratio

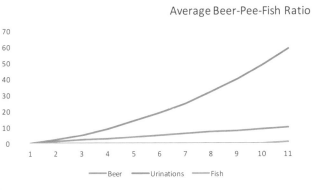

THE BANANA MYTH

Bananas are considered bad luck on a fishing boat by many captains. There is a basis for this belief. It may be a myth, but it can influence your catch.

The bad luck theory of **bananas** is derived from the misfortune of stevedores unloading banana boats from Central America. The cargo most often contained biting spiders that not only were painful, but occasionally deadly. **Stevedores** considered it bad luck to be assigned to unloading a banana boat. This is the truth behind the myth. **

This would drive any stevadore to walk the plank

The effect that this superstition has on anglers is real. As you know, **Karma** is very important. The mere thought of bad luck can cause an imbalance in the captain and/or crew's **Yin and Yang**. The imbalance results in a **poor catch**. Bananas are bad luck only for those who believe they are bad luck. However, one superstitious crewmember can affect an entire boat's Karma.

** This is actually true

FACT FILES:

Fish are repelled by pheromones and pick up the scent from miles.
This is the reason women aren't often seen on fishing expeditions.

IF THE COWS ARE STANDING, THE FISH ARE BITING

It is said to be attributed to Neptune, the mythological Roman God of Water and the sea. Neptune also happened to be worshipped by the Romans as a god of horses, under the name "Neptune Equester."*

His connection between the sea and land was eminent, and the legend was once said to read *'if the horses are running, the fish are biting.'* Indian fisherman, versed in Hinduism learned of this and supplanted the horse with the sacred cow, the symbol of abundance, selfless giving and a full earthly life, adapting the interpretation to fit their beliefs. The alteration may have had something to do with the very limited numbers of horses in India, causing frustration to fisherman.

History has shown **the cows relationship with the sea is just as accurate as the horse**, as depicted in the Fishma Sutra.

If you really want to be sure, The Holy reading instructs to check two or three paddocks, remembering, the closer the paddock to the water, the more accurate.

*This is actually a fact.

Artistic depiction from the Fishma Sutra of the legend at work.
It appears if the cow's are standing, the fish are biting!

CHAPTER 16

7 THINGS YOU DIDN'T KNOW ABOUT FISHING

Fishing has influenced man more than you know. We explore a few ways in which the act of catchin' the little critters has helped their superior cousins

*legal disclaimer... just like the rest of this book, this chapter is fictional.

1 The 'boat' dates back to biblical times, but it is seldom known the real reason for it's invention.

Proven time and time again, most inventions were born out of necessity, the boat is no different. The first Anglers and Danglers, whom fished not just for recreation, but for survival, grew frustrated that human abilities limited them to fishing the immediate area close to the shore.

Aware of the schools of fish the greater ocean offered they set about creating a way to replicate their stability on land whilst being out on the water. Earlier models are believed to be very basic, more like a raft, but cemented the **principles of flotation** still followed by todays commercial liners.

The now popular arc shaped hull became trendy after it's first and very successful voyage, under **Captain Noah**. Credited as being the most successful hunting and gathering trip in history, story has it that two of every species on Earth were caught. The **great storm of 500 B.C.** was only survived by two craft, both having a significant impact on fishing over time. The other, became the reason for the birth of the now tradition of christening boats (see Boating, Chapter 10 pg.67).

2 **A**nother interesting fact about fishing is it's profound influence on the arts over the years, namely *song lyrics*. It is indeed interesting to learn the original versions of popular songs showed they were *tales of heartache and love... of fishing*. *Such songs as Kenny Roger's 'The Gambler' (The Angler), Bon Jovi's 'It's My Life', U2's 'Beautiful Day' and The Beatles' 'Hard Days Night' are amongst those originally sung about the old golden recreation (see Glossary for full lyrics) pg. 101).

This little guy really took to the lessons. Kinda gives new meaning to when Bryan Adams said 'I got my first real six string...'

The Beatles loved fishing, so much so it inspired their hit song 'Hard Day's Night'. Rumours have it their record company made them change the lyrics to suit a 'wider' audience

4 **T:** The *Dead Fish Flop* (also known as *The Dying Fish*), is the sporadic thrust-like motion a fish makes whilst sitting on ice in the boat. This happens when the nervous systems 'postmen' - neurons, instinctively send signals via electrochemical waves throughout the body in a last ditch effort to catapult itself back into its natural habitat. The *Dying Fish* is now recognised as an official sexual manoeuvre in the *Karma Sutra*.

3 **F**ishing has also aided in music education, with teachers now using adaptations from old seadogs sayings to help students in the learning process. The fishing communities widespread motto, *Every Good Boy Deserves Fish*, made into an acronym, *EGBDF*, was found to represent the notes of the musical stave and taught to kids so they would remember it by having a reference point. Another example saw teachers struggling to get through to fishing loving kids at a school in the remote fishing village of Pullet-In, Thailand, come up with the saying '*Every Angler Dangles Gracefully But Effectively*', to help students remember the strings on a guitar *(EADGBE)*.

THE MODERN
KARMA SUTRA

5 **F**ish are still used as ***currency*** in many countries. There are many fraudulent copies found, but authentic ones have *'legal tender'* tattooed behind the poop hole, and a hologram noticeable when held at an angle of 37° to the sun, just under the gill's.

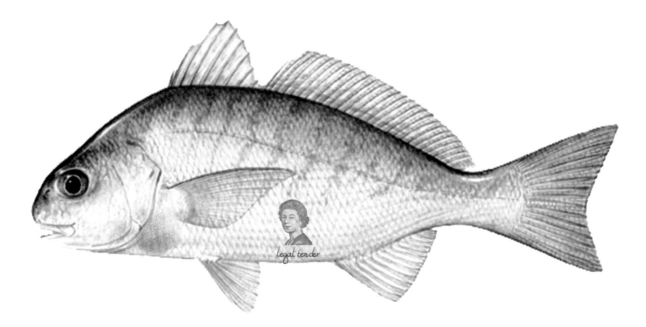

legal tender

6 **T**he *natural compass* Fish contain a trace element of Mercury, and hence they contain certain magnetic qualities, meaning when idol and not affected by currents or exerting physical effort, they will naturally tend to ***magnetic north***. Ever wonder how Captains could navigate with a broken compass?

7 **T**he tarpaulin as we know it was designed to replicate the skin of a fish. The weave of the tarp imitates the scales to give it a waterproof and sleek finish.

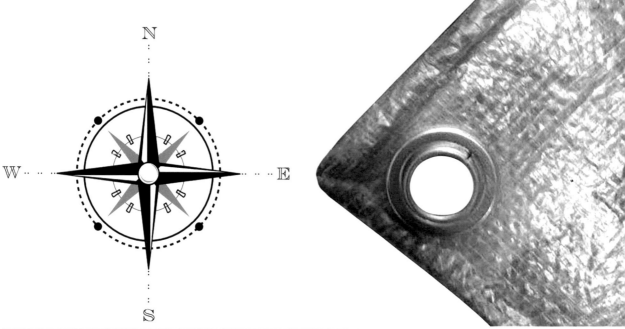

CHAPTER 17

1 MORE THING YOU DIDN'T KNOW ABOUT FISHING

CHEFRIDOLOGY CHART

The science of *Chefridology,* developed by our in-house celebrity chef and Dr. of Food *Reno Grigio*, works on the knowledge that patterns, colours, and other characteristics of the fishes *iris* hold information about how to best prepare, season, cook and serve that fish.

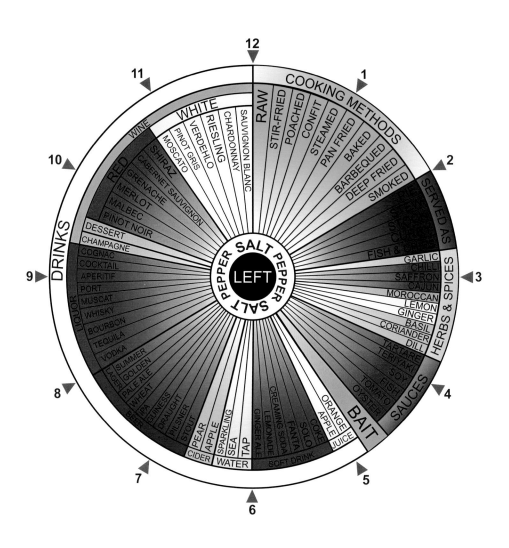

IRIS ZONES

- BEER
- SERVED AS
- WATER, COOKING METHODS
- SAUCES, RED WINE
- LIQUOR, SOFT DRINK
- WHITE WINE, JUICE
- CIDER, HERBS AND SPICES

Reno says the best way to do this is once you have your catch, look into the fishes eyes, both left and right and note down any patterns - spots or dashes, and dis-colourations that exist. Then cross reference that with his in depth diagram and voila... you have the best cooking methods, seasoning, and even beverage choices to complement your catch.

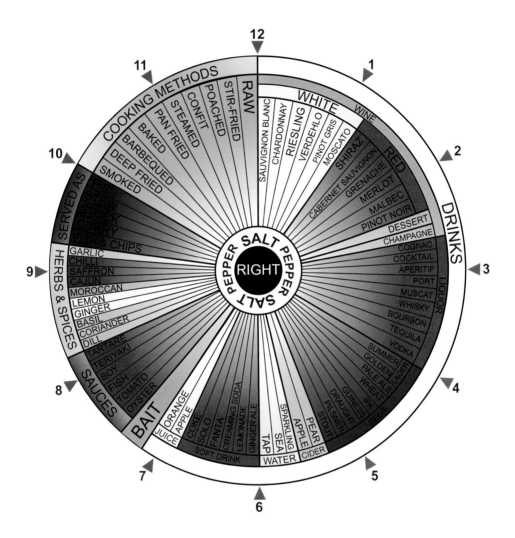

Developed by Reno Grigio, Ph. D. from Barossa Correctional Centre
www.renogrigio/cell12/prison/eyeofthefish/chefridology.com

DEFINITIONS
SOME BASIC FISHING TERMS

ROD:

1. A man's name short for Rodney

2. Common name for a purpose built straight-line sprint race care. 'Hot-Rod'

3. Willy, schlong, johnson, member or penis

4. A pole used in fishing

LINE:

1. A type of dance

2. To 'draw a line in the sand'

3. A design element. ie. Line, Point etc..

4. A strong material used for fishing

PORT:

1. The fortified stuff mostly enjoyed by older and wiser fishermen. Ideal with cheese and grapes, and perfect for a night cap

2. The left side of a boat or ship

3. Where you park your boat

STARBOARD:

1. Is the place where a legend is celebrated by having their name and achievements printed on some form of public display

2. The right side of a boat or ship

Wacko Jacko sitting Starboard

BOW:

1. Act of bending at the hip to mark the end of a performance, often in gratitude for the audiences applause. 'To take a bow'

2. The front of your boat

STERN:

1. Serious and unrelenting, especially in the assertion of authority

2. The back of your boat

THE ONE THAT GOT AWAY:

- The one you always pictured getting that photo with for the family albums. Came so close... but never hooked her

KEEPER:

- The one that fell for your line and was brought on-board

Good shot here of a keeper!

ORIGINAL LYRICS TO KENNY ROGER'S 'THE ANGLER'

On a warm summer's evenin' on a boat bound for nowhere
I met up with The Angler we were both to tired to speak
So we took turns a starin' over the water at the darkness
'til barely a bite was had… and he began to speak

He said, "Son I've made a life, out of fishin' this old sea bed
And knowin' where the fish swam and what they want to eat
So if you don't mind me sayin, I can see your out of bait boy,
for a can of your VB, like King's we shall eat"

So I handed him a tinnie, and he drank it to the bottom
Than he bummed a sinker, and asked me for a knife
And the night got deathly quiet, but you could hear the tuna jumpin
If you gonna learn to cast a line out you gotta learn to cast it right

You gotta know when they hatchin' know where to catch 'em
know when to cast a line… and let it run
You never count your takings in front of the lady
If you gonna learn to tell a story you gotta learn to tell it right

Now every angler knows that the secret to a story is knowin' what to photograph,
and what to delete cos every casts a winner and every casts a loser
if you gonna learn to tell a story you gotta tell it right.

You gotta know when they hatchin' know where to catch 'em know when to cast a line… and
let it run
You never count your takings in front of the lady
If you gonna learn to tell a story you gotta learn to tell it right

101

ORIGINAL LYRICS TO U2'S 'BEAUTIFUL DAY'

You're out of luck
The tides gone and you're still out here
The boat is stuck
And you're not movin anywhere

You haven't caught a thing
But you don't lose faith
It goes hand in hand with Zen
Karma and good bait

It's a Beautiful Day
The line casts it feels like
It's a Beautiful Day
Don't let it get away

You're on a boat, in the middle of the ocean,
you're out of bait, and you need some suntan lotion...
Life is good... even if you haven't caught a thing
You've fished for hours... it's time to catch a few

It's a Beautiful Day
The line casts it feels like
It's a Beautiful Day
Don't let 'em get away

See the water it's green and blue
See dolphins right in front of you
See the skyline broken by cloud
See the Great Whites scaring surfers out
See the illuminescent fish at night
See the tuna fleets at first light
See the fish with hook in its mouth

After the burley... they all came out
Dayyyyyyyyyyy...

It's a Beautiful Day
The line casts it feels like
It's a Beautiful Day
Don't let 'em get away

ORIGINAL LYRICS TO BON JOVI'S 'IT'S MY LIFE'

This ain't a fish for the average angler
No silent fight no good for dangler's
I ain't gonna be just a rod in the boat
They're gonna feel my hook
I'm gonna make them float

Its My Life
Its now or never
I just wanna fish forever
I just wanna fish while I'm alive
(It's My Life)
The sea is like an open highway
Like Rex Hunt said I'll fish it my way
I just wanna fish while I'm alive
It's my life

This is for the one whose still in bed
My lovely lady, restin' her head
Tomorrows gonna be such a seafood fest
I promised her I'd bring her back

The oceans best
Its My Life
Its now or never
I just wanna fish forever
I just wanna fish while I'm alive
(It's My Life)
The sea is like an open highway
Like ET said I'll fish it my way
I just wanna fish while I'm alive
It's my life

ORIGINAL LYRICS THE BEATLES' 'HARD DAY'S NIGHT'

It's been a hard days night
I've been fishin' like a dog
It's been a hard days night
Yeah I caught me a big log

But when I get home to you
And you serve it as food
You know I feel alright

You know I fish all day
To keep you healthy & fed well
I love it when I hear you say
That me fishing rings your bell

But when I get on my boat
And I start to float
You know I'm fishin' for you..

When I float
And when I feel a big bight.. bight.. bight
When I float
What will we eat tonight... yeah

GLOSSARY

THE A-Z OF FISHING

A – Anglin', Antique Fish, AAESTCF

B – Bearded Clam, Birds Nest

C - Chappelli

D – Danglin', Drag n Snag, Depth Finder

E – Every Good Boy Deserves Fish

F – Fake Lines Up, Fishnets

G – Granny Knot, Gumboot Fish

H – Horn Fish, Half-Windsor, Hippy Fish

I – I Roy McCoy, choose fishing as my one true love

J – Jagged Rockfish

K – Karma

L – Lumber Jack, Logfish, Lines-Up

M – Mixed Grill

N – Noose, N for Nelly

O – Oh f*%k, hope you can swim

P - Plugs

Q - Quantity over quality

R – Ring-Pull Method

S – Sea Sickness, Schnozza, Spanish Lady, Silverfish, Starfish, Scorpion

T – Trenching, Truckies Hitch, Tango

U – Umbrella Fish

V – Very big fish

W – Windsor Knot, WANCAS

X - Xylophone

Y – Yellow-Fin Tuna

Z - Zen

Cheers and beers...

Thank you's

only plan on writing one book in this life - so I want to make sure I get this bit right, because it's important. Very few things happen in life without the help of others.... and I have been fortunate to get a lot of help from some great people to help my vision come to life.

To Bill Classon, Debbie, Julian and the publishing team at AFN (Australian Fishing Network). You took this book on and I am very grateful for that. I can't guarantee it will be a best seller, but I guarantee I will be proud of the product and I hope you will look back with a smile and be happy that it's in the AFN stable. Jules thanks for your design wizardry.

Of course a big thank you goes to the ***real Barry and Roy - Terry and Lehmo.***

Terry you were all in from the first time I called and spoke to you about it, and this exemplifies why you are the perfect Barry Jeffreys. Thanks for being so generous with your time, it is truly appreciated. I look forward to our next beer.

Lehmo - it was great having your comedic influence come through in your character. You have been wonderful to work with and I really appreciate you becoming invested in the project.

I have also had fun getting in touch with and meeting a lot of great Australians who are mentioned or feature in the book. Thanks to them all for being great sports. **Rex Hunt, John Bertrand (AO), Matthew Hayden, Andrew Symonds, ET, Mark Berg, Dick Johnson, The Arden St Anglers, Merv Hughes, Dermott Brereton, Paddy Dangerfield, Mark LeCras, Jack Wighton and Jai Taurima.**

Yannas (Michelle Yann) - You helped bring the book to life with your creativity and graphic talent and I cannot thank you enough. Your ability to understand some pretty different concepts and get them out of my head and onto paper has brought me great joy, and was significant in the book sprouting from seed to plant.

Harv - an incredibly talented artist, who nailed the cover and cartoon fillers and understood the exact vibe of the book. Thanks mate, it has made a huge impact in conveying the tone of the book.

My team of editors and helpers

Benny D - thanks mate, you have a great sense for what works and I appreciate your help when it was needed.

Dave Rosser - massive help to me. Also, it was great sending grabs to you for a good ego boost. We have the same sense of humour so I knew you'd always get it. Thanks for the editing - I still haven't mastered when to use apostrophes' ;)

Janny D - Joy McCoy's biggest fan.

Brother Hoze - for teaching me the stages of sea sickness, and everything else you've done.

Zippy - a better mate is hard to find.

Simmo - cheers mate.

Cam from Tam - After you read the book Cam I was truly inspired to finish it and get it published because of your enthusiasm. It gave me great joy to see someone enjoy my book so much - I thank you for that.

Richard Hearn & Rhys Bennett for your cameos.

David Bell for lending your boat for a quick picture with Tez.

Big Anthony & the lads at 'Finding Joe' for the Lean n' Grab picture.

Nigie for your naked photos bracing that fish. Thought we would've needed a bigger fish.

Pete - the Barry to my Roy, who could forget that fateful fishing trip with your old man and brother. It really formed the idea of the book. And thanks for the fishnet pictures - great pins.

Mum & Dad - I'm grateful that you instilled in me a good sense of humility and sense of humour, and also encouraged us to pursue our ambitions in life however ridiculous they may seem... like this book.

Nealo (Daniher) - I was fortunate to fall in love with your daughter & you've proven to be a very adequate father-in-law!

Thanks Nealo, you opened some doors for me which really helped make this book happen. I really owe you a lot.

And of course my beautiful wife Bec ♥

You are just an amazing and strong woman. Your understanding and encouragment while I worked on this project... night after night after night after night won't be forgotten.

You balance my abstractness which in-turn creates a balance I may not have otherwise. I am a better man with you by my side. Thanks for all you do. Can I get another boat?

Drew

ABOUT THE AUTHOR

Drew Howell, grew up in Orange, NSW, some 300 kilometres from the nearest ocean, and it's fair to say fishing wasn't his natural go to. But the lack of ocean didn't stop this country boy from cultivating a good sense of humility and a love for the quintessential Aussie send up style of humour he grew up with.

Not a great fisherman by his own admission but one who loves the adventure, and far more importantly, sees the comedy in the calamity of a fisherman down on his luck or a trip that doesn't go quite to plan.

Howell, a well educated and well rounded lad has travelled the world and broadened his views through living and seeing some of the most unique cultures, and breathtaking sites the earth has to offer. But it was the draw of the golden shores of the 'lucky country', and that familiar Aussie larrikin culture that brought him home.

After a fishing trip to North QLD with mates exposed some 'deficiencies' in their fishing skill set, Drew set about creating this book to capture all of those laughable moments. The next job; craft some characters whose self-inflated confidence oozes like that of the classic Aussie 'weekend warrior' Dad we are all familiar with, with a touch of sporting legend thrown in for good measure paying homage to the likes of Rex Hunt and ET.

Howell relates his comedic writing style and characters back to influences of Aussie comedy greats Glenn Robbins, Mick Molloy, Tom Gleisner et al, with a splash of Will Ferrell outrageousness. His satirical take on an Aussie fishing guide draws parallels with the publication style of West-Queensland based parody print 'The Betoota Advocate', and Working Dog's 'Jetlag Travel Guides' and chronicles the perceived culture of fishing as much as it does the actual means.

Drew says... "I have crossed many things off the list in my life by the age of 36, and let me tell you, I am bloody proud to be able to say I'm a published author. I really hope anyone who reads my book gets the purposeful idiocy with which it is meant. It's ridiculous, it's light, it's fun. Life is too short and far too serious. Do me a favour, put your worries aside when you pick up The Idiots Guide to Anglin' & Danglin' and feel free to have a laugh **at** Barry and Roy - my two lovable larrikins."

Drew now resides in Melbourne with his wife Bec, and owns two more boats then she would like. He is looking forward to raising a young family, so one day his kids can pick-up this book and have a chuckle as much at their old man as Barry and Roy.